Binderella
Almost a Fairy Tale

Binderella
Almost a Fairy Tale

By: Ben Isaac

City Point Books
Yulee, Florida

BINDERELLA Almost a Fairy Tale

By Ben Isaac

Published by:
City Point Books
P.O. Box 221
Yulee, Florida 32041
benjaminisaac@bellsouth.net

CITY POINT BOOKS are available at special discounts for bulk purchases, sales promotions, fund raising or educational purposes.

ISBN#: 978-0-615-27021-0

Library of Congress Control Number: 2008912233

Dedication

This story is dedicated to the Board of Directors. It is with the help of this unorganized Board that the project was brought to fruition. These people made a much more powerful impact than the fairy godmother did in Cinderella's case. In fact, this Board's job had many more difficulties.

The members of this Board of Directors are as follows: Jesse Taylor Simmons Isaac, Walter Isaac, Sallie Hollings, Lillie Mae Richardson Isaac, Ivory Isaac, Helen Simmons, Robinson Wynn, Benjamin Taylor, Carolyn Popkins, Richard Blake, Jonah Mack Isaac, Robert Omeara, Robert Hitchell, Thomas Lee Isaac, Benjamin A. Morse, and Leara Bell Means Zellner Richardson.

Now, the work of these people is neither a unified nor an organized effort to do a certain job. In fact, most of these folks did not know one another. Still, as a whole, these people did so very much to inspire, motivate, stimulate and save Bindie's life from a terrible ruin. Just imagine some of the illegal troubles he could have gotten into without the Board's directions. However, let's not forget, negative acts can help if one allows them to do so.

—Caasi Neb

Acknowledgements

I thank the following individuals for their help, support and encouragement in completing this project: Lillie Mae Isaac, Yvonne Rose, and Amber Communications Group, Inc., Ginny Selley Ginny and Dorothy Hughes at the Gateway Bookstore (Jacksonville).

Table of Contents

Prelude

There are at least three outstanding facts about this story, which many people will probably agree. First, there is a great deal of hate and evil in this world. Second, it takes more than one parent or person to raise a child. The third fact I speak of will become very obvious as you read the pages of this story.

This is the story of Bindie, as he is called, along with many other much less flattering (ugly) names. However, Bindie is the short name for Binderella... no, not Cinderella... Binderella.

Binderella

Introduction

*Y*es, my name is Binderella. No, this is not a fairy tale. I am a real live individual. However, many times in my life experiences, it seems a bit surreal. You may think that is true when you read this story.

I don't have any stepsisters or stepbrothers. I do have some half-sisters and half-brothers. In spite of that, I can earnestly tell you that stepsisters or stepbrothers could not be any meaner than some of my half-sisters, half-brothers and one of my whole brothers.

I do have two whole brothers, and one of them seems more like a stepbrother. In fact, I have not considered the term stepbrother before. However, most of the times it really did feel like my older whole brother, Tarmmy, (not my oldest whole brother but the one next to me in age), was like my stepbrother. Most of the time, if my dad or my oldest whole brother were not around, it felt just like he was stepping on me.

I am the youngest child, and most of the time it really felt like all of my mom's children were stepping on me, except one. My whole brother, Ivee, was very caring and helpful. Still, it felt like the rest of mom's children were stepping on me and putting me down, most of the time.

"Sticks and stones may break your bones, but words will never hurt you." I don't know who first wrote that quote, but it is a lie. I know, because I have some wounds from the words. That is why the Board deserves a hearty "thank you" and congratulations for the work, time, and investment of love and care most of these people have brought to my life. Yes, this is the Board of Directors of the corporation that helped produce this person called Binderella.

Oh, yes, it took all of these people listed as my "Board of Directors" and more, to help me make my life as successful as it is. They all had a hand in shaping my life. That may seem like a prideful statement, but it is not a statement of pride at all. To me, a prideful statement would be: "I achieved all of my accomplishments by myself and on my own efforts, with no help."

Nevertheless, let me tell you right here that every member of this Board did not mean well. But remember the old adage, "If you are given a sour lemon, make lemonade." I like lemonade; no, I love lemonade.

Now, let me present to you the almost fairy tale of Binderella. For those of you who have read and forgotten that old fairy tale of Cinderella, as you read these pages, the tale will come back to your memory. This story begins way down south in the land of sunshine. It is the southernmost portion of the country.

Cast of Characters

1. Bessie Ivory

2. Walter Ivory

3. Callie Hollings

4. Mae Ivory

5. Ivee Ivory

6. Elena Simms Hobinson

7. Lenjamin Taylor

8. Carolyn Popkins

9. Richard Lake

10. Johnny Mack Ivory

11. Tobert Comeara

12. Robert Hitchell

13. Tarmmy Lee Ivory

14. Hinjamin Norse

15. Cleara Bell Binjamin

Part One

Binderella's Family

Once upon a time, there was a little African-American boy. He lived in a little village named City Point. This little boy's name is Binderella, albeit, everyone calls him Bindie.

Chapter I

Mom

First, Binderella has to give tribute and thanks to his mom. Thank God she was not an abortionist or I would not have been here at all. If she had been, perhaps I would have been partially here.

I am also grateful to mom for the encouragement she has given me in my life. I am so very thankful for the timely reassurance she gave in my pre-teenage years. Yes, it is true I was only three years old when mom died.

In spite of all that, I have some feelings and no doubt of the love she had for me. In fact, I have only two very distinct instances which I remember my mother's appearance in my life.

The first time was at my mom's funeral. There was lots of crying and excitement, but I was simply puzzled by all that was happening. It was very difficult, no, impossible, for this three-year-old to understand death. That was particularly true since nobody was explaining to me what was happening. There was one significant fact, however. Everybody there loved my mom very much. She meant a lot to many people.

Meanwhile, through the years, I have learned that some people were upset with Mom for leaving her first husband and marrying my dad.

Mainly, these were Joe Simms' children. Nonetheless, their feelings are very understandable unless Mom was going through some things that these children of Joe Simms did not know.

Mom was not about to tell Joe's children that she was being mistreated. I can very well understand Mom not wanting to tell her children that their dad abused her. She feared that would make them hate their dad. However, the older children had heard and knew about the abuse, but they did not mention it. That was an awful situation at the very least.

On the other hand, I am getting ahead of myself about Mom. Her story does not begin in Gifford, Florida. It begins in Greensville, Florida, the same Greensville where Ray Charlie's grandparents lived, yes, the "Ray Charlie."

Grandpa Will and Grandma Ida had three children, Aunt Maggie, uncle Bin, and my mom, Bessie. Somehow they all ended up in Brevard County. Aunt Maggie and Mom lived next to each other until Mom died.

Meanwhile, as soon as the funeral was over, I felt the chill of cold treatment from my relatives. You know, if a three-year-old child can feel it, no doubt it was really chilly. It was as if they could not wait to show my dad and me how much they hated us. Still, in all of this, my dad seemed to be very calm. He held his peace. Dad seemed to accept the circumstances with resolve and with emotional and stoic calmness.

My mom left a total of ten children when she died. We ranged in age from three to twenty years old. It took me years to find out that my mom died while trying to give birth to her eleventh child. Neither she nor the baby lived. Since I was an adult when I found out the cause of Mom's death, and I was not the last pregnancy, it occurred to me I could have been the cause of her death. It could have been my fault.

Maybe that was the reason for all the anger and hate I had been feeling aimed at me. It is so very unfair for a child not to be given this kind of information. Of course, I am sure that this refusal to share this fact was not done intentionally. The fact remains that it was a heavy burden for a child to bear unnecessarily.

I am partly to blame, since I never asked my dad to explain to me what happened to cause Mom's early death. She was only forty-two years old. For sure, Dad would have told me if I had asked.

Chapter II

Dad

My dad was a fair and caring man, much more caring than I could tell in my very early years. After all, he took care of his three boys who were under the age of twelve. He did not complain, fuss, or argue over anything that would not hurt us in some way. He also made sure we had a place to live, food to eat, and clothes to wear. That job was not nearly as easy when I was a child, as it is today.

I have sixteen sisters and brothers. Yes, this is a family of his, hers, and theirs. We are very well distributed. Dad had one child by his first wife. Lillie is my oldest sister. Although I have never seen her, I have met her daughter.

Dad's first wife died very soon after Lillie was born. He then moved from Alabama to Georgia. While living in Georgia, Dad met and married his second wife. Dad and his second wife had six children together; however, Dad had to leave Albany, Georgia under certain pressures. When he left Albany, he moved to Florida. When my dad moved to Florida, he left his seven children in Georgia. After some time, he met Mom, and they got married. When they got together, they had three children; however, this did not happen as soon as he left Albany, Georgia.

Walter Ivory, my dad, was a fantastic, incredibly gifted individual. He was a laborer with an overload of vision and foresight. He had only a ninth-grade education. Nevertheless, he had a great appreciation of what a person can accomplish. It amazes me how the man could see through all of that mass of negativity and put downs of his generation and keep his vision of what each individual could do with his or her life, even though he never knew a Bob Hitchell (we'll meet Bob later).

Mr. Ivory, my dad, worked hard and studied more. One of his favorite quotes was "man works from sun to sun (sun-up to sun-down), and a woman's work is never done." There were many sayings like that. Another one of his favorites was "an idle mind and idle hands is the devil's workshop." Therefore, needless to say, he kept his three boys busy working.

My dad was a very complicated individual. He had a sense of pride in his academic achievement. However, Walter Ivory was one of the most humble persons I have ever known. He would help you in any way he could, and he was not devious. If he could not help you, he would not do anything to hurt you. Dad also did what he had to do in order to take care of his three sons who were less than twelve years old when our mom died.

First of all, my dad was a very strict disciplinarian. He demanded and got respect from his three sons. He also made sure that his sons respected other adults.

Although Dad was humble and helpful, he had some problems. He was in no way perfect. Dad left a wife and seven children behind in Georgia when he moved to Florida. Yes, he made mistakes, also.

With all the knowledge and wisdom that Dad possessed, he did not realize our society was not ready for equal rights' laws to be put on the books in the south in the early 1920's. So he tried to preach equal rights in the black community. However, his white Georgia neighbors would not hear of it. Consequently, his very life was threatened. So his

brother had to bring him to Florida in a coffin. This was not so difficult since his brother was a funeral director or an undertaker.

This next phase of Dad's life has always puzzled me. Dad left Albany,
Georgia to get away from white people. Then he moved to Holipaw,
Florida. There are only white people in Holipaw, Florida. Still, Dad
must have known what he was doing, because he stayed in Holipaw
for years without any trouble. While he was in Holipaw, Florida, he
worked on the railroad.

However, this whole episode destroyed Bindie's (my) theory about
why I know Jesus was African. When Joseph and Mary were hiding
the baby Jesus, they took him to Egypt. It would seem impossible to
hide a white baby Jesus in an African nation. Nevertheless, if my dad,
Walter Ivory, could hide out in Holipaw, Florida, I know a white Jesus
could have hidden in an African nation. Still, both incidents seem a
bit unreal and creepy.

Meanwhile, it is still a mystery to me as to why my dad did these
extremes. He moved from Holipaw, Florida to Gifford, Florida. Now,
while Holipaw was all white people, Gifford was all African Americans. It was as if he was studying both cultures.

The only thing that makes sense to me about him leaving Holipaw is
that someone white from Albany, Georgia went to Holipaw, and after
recognizing Dad, he or she said, "Hol-lee-paw! That is Walter Ivory!"
So Dad decided to move on. He decided to move to the east coast of
Florida. Therefore, he ended up in Gifford. Now, Gifford was kind of
unique. It was one of those twin towns in Florida. The other twin was
Vero Beach, Florida. However, these were not identical twins. Gifford
was all African Americans, while Vero Beach was all Caucasians.

In Gifford, my dad met and fell in love with my mom who was to
become his third wife. When Dad met my mom, she was already
married to Joseph Simms.

Some of my brothers and sisters say that Mr. Ivory was the cause of Mr. and Mrs. Joseph Simms' separation. However, there are other accounts of why mom left Joe Simms. Some of the anecdotes, my sisters and brothers will not face up to. It is convenient for them to put the blame on my dad.

I feel like Mom was smarter than my brothers and sisters were willing to give her credit for. Here is a woman who has a happy home and family who she loves. But that is not enough. She leaves this loving home and goes off and marries another man who has nothing to offer her. There simply has to be more to the story. While in Gifford, Mom gave birth to her eighth child. His name is Ivee.

Nevertheless, Besse and Walter left Gifford, Florida and moved to Brevard County, Florida. They settled in a little place called Merritt Island, which is due west of Cape Canaveral, Florida. Merritt Island is located between the Banana River and the Indian River in Brevard County. Mom and Dad moved there after Ivee was born in Gifford.

Three years later, Mom had her ninth baby. His name is Tarmmy. Both of these brothers were born in the month of December. For some reason, I always wondered if these were Mom's Christmas gifts to Dad. Ivee was born a week after Christmas, and Tarmmy was born two days before Christmas. Of course, I never got the opportunity to ask Mom.

This couple's third child was Binderella. They must have both been surprised, because Bindie's parents were both older at that time. Not only that, but Mom was now a divorced mom with ten children.

Life was very difficult for Mom and Dad. Still, they made a living and took care of these children. Even after Mom died, Dad continued to take care of the boys. Of course, he had help just as every single parent needs, even today.

However, as stated, Dad was a strong and firm disciplinarian. He believed very firmly in having and giving respect. All three of us knew that we must have and give respect to everyone.

Not only was my dad a good provider who gave as well as asked for respect, he was a giving man. Now, I don't want to deceive anyone. Dad did not have a lot to give away since we lived in extreme poverty. Nevertheless, my dad could read and write well. While that may not seem to be a big deal in today's world, when I was a child, it was a very big deal.

You see, when I was a child, the education level in my African American community where I grew up was, on average, below fifth grade level. It was not unusual to see someone who had never been to school. Then, there were so many adults who could not read at all.

This was not the case with my dad. He had completed the ninth grade. In some places, a person could teach elementary school if he or she had finished eighth grade. Dad could read very well. He had been encouraged and inspired to get a good education. Dad met a person who had authored a book or two, and this man became a mentor to my father. Dad learned an awful lot from this man. Dad never forgot his mentor. Dad mentioned him often and gave him praise.

My dad showed his gratitude in many ways. First of all, he was always trying to help someone else. It seemed that his daily task, after his retirement, was to do a good deed for someone. Dad would do almost any job, from teaching a person to read, to plowing a field and planting vegetables. He simply liked to see things grow. He would help if he could help them grow anything from hogs in a pen to Hibiscus in a yard. He liked seeing children mature properly into adults.

There was only this one situation that seemed to make Dad angry. He would get very upset by the lack of respect, especially when children were disrespecting adults. That was the one case in which my dad would lose control. He had a real problem with that. Dad would lose his temper and sometimes lose his judgment about what was enough discipline. No, he was not perfect; however, he did take care of his three sons.

While I remember my dad in the village of City Point, I can think of only one man in that village to compare him with. That man's name was Games Phoster. Mr. Phoster was an auto mechanic in City Point. He was the best mechanic in the whole area. However, being the best auto mechanic was not the only thing that made him so well known. The reason Mr. Phoster stands out in my memory is because of something else. Mr. Phoster loved to talk about and discuss philosophy. That is why he reminds me of my father.

Dad also loved to discuss philosophical and theological ideas. In fact, even today not many people like to discuss the works of Josephus. Dad enjoyed talking about the works of Josephus. The problem was he did not have anyone with whom he could talk about Josephus. You see, during Dad's days, the people he was talking to thought he was talking about Mary's husband Joseph. They thought he was talking about Jesus' earthly dad.

I am sure that it was a terribly lonely existence for him, much of the time. He literally had nobody to discuss philosophy and theology with him. However, Dad, who my brothers and sisters called Mr. Izieke (Ivory), did not seem to show this loneliness. He did a lot for his neighbors. He was especially good and helpful to his neighbors who needed a handyman. It seemed to give him so much joy to help someone with a job that the person himself or herself could not do.

In that way, Dad and Aunt Callie were very similar. It was like they were brother and sister. There did not seem to be a need for any financial reward for these two people. Both of them seemed to have received so much joy from seeing the appreciation expressed by neighbors who received their help.

Life went on this way with Dad for many, many years. Dad worked hard and was paid very little, even when he was working for money. He would do work and get paid by the job rather than by the hour.

In fact, the most money my dad was paid was when we would dig up old dead fruit trees. The grove owners would want to replace the dead trees in the grove with young, live trees. So they would pay my dad one dollar a tree for every tree we would dig up. The most I can remember us digging up was thirteen trees one day. Still, it would take all four of us to dig up one tree.

This is the type of hard work that caused my older whole brothers to leave home. After my two older brothers left home, my dad and I continued to do these types of jobs. Then something happened that made us stop these jobs.

Dad got a bad infection in his right leg. Then the infection became worse. It became so serious that Dad could no longer get out of bed. The infection moved up Dad's legs to his thigh. Then his disease moved into his abdomen.

Consequently, my dad's health began to deteriorate. He would have good days and bad days. Still, on his good days, he could not get out of bed. So the job of taking care of Dad became progressively more difficult.

I mentioned earlier that my mother had an influential impact on my life two times. The first time was at her funeral. Just to see so many people grieving over her was overwhelming, even at that early age. The second time Mom appeared to me was even more startling. I was facing a crisis.

My father was very ill, and I was his caretaker. Now, an eleven-year-old is not so competent to handle a medical crisis. One day Dad was having a very difficult time. So I stayed with him all that day and stayed up with him all that night. In the early morning the next day, Dad was beginning to get much worse. So about 3:30 a.m. that morning I had to go to get my older sister to come help with my dad. She lived a little over a mile from us.

On the way there, as I passed the house where Mom died, a lady approached me. This lady came up to me, and I was tearfully face to face with my mom. She said, "Son, everything is going to be fine. I promise, Bindie." She told me convincingly that Dad would be all right now. She also assured me that my life will be good and all will go well, later. Just as suddenly as she appeared, she disappeared. However, as Mom vanished from my sight, I felt much better about everything. Sure enough I went and got my sister, and we returned to my dad. She did some therapy of some sort on my dad. Whatever she did for Dad, it worked. Dad quickly began feeling better. That was a very surreal experience with my mom that morning. Close to ten years after her death, Mom consoled and inspired me.

Chapter III

Sister Elena

My sister, Elena, had been taking some correspondence nursing courses. Therefore, she knew some basic nursing practices, which an eleven-year-old boy had no knowledge of how to do or even what to do.

When Elena finished, my dad went to sleep. Then I went to sleep. My sister returned to her home. My dad then slept most of that day. There was no school for me that day either.

While writing about this incident, it is still an emotional and tearful account in my life. I can only say it was a heartfelt and lonely-filled few hours in my life that I cannot forget. My mom and her love and my sister and all of her bedside manners, along with her nursing skills, were a strong emotional and comforting occurrence in my life.

The lady who gave me life and the sister, who I later lived with for ten years, both impacted my life in a heartfelt moment, or rather for a couple of hours that somehow seemed much longer.

After that day, my life seemed to be going much smoother. My routine was less confusing and frustrating. I would go to school and concentrate on my schoolwork rather than worry about Dad. Before this time, I was missing something in my school days most of the time. However, now, I could go to school and actually study with full focus and then return home without any tears, most everyday.

Elena started a new routine also. Once or twice a week she would come by our home to see how Dad was doing. That gave me a lot more relief just to know she would be coming by at least once a week to check on Dad.

Then one day during the summer, everything changed for the worse for Dad and me. I heard something one morning while I was sleeping. That sound awakened me. It seemed like a bright, sunny morning in July; however, I noticed Dad was having difficulty breathing. I went to him and tried to talk to him. I asked him what was wrong, but there was no response. I kept trying to get him to respond to me, but he would not. So after a minute or so I ran out the door to go get my sister; however, when I started down the road, I saw her husband's car coming towards me. I waved him down, because I knew he would not stop if I did not wave for him to stop.

Meanwhile, my sister was in the car with him. Elena wanted to know what was wrong. I told her I could not get Dad to respond to me. I told her I thought he was in pain; however, he was just making a gurgling noise in the back of his mouth. Elena came into the house and removed the pillow from under Dad's head. Then he started to quiet down some. After that she asked me if we had some Epsom salt, and I said, no. So she told me to go to the store and get some Epsom salt. She said her husband was going to stay there in case they had to take Dad to the hospital.

Reluctantly, I went to the store, but I did not want to go. Elena realized Dad was dying. I did not know that Dad had asked Elena not to let me be there at his death. So I went to the store very upset that she would send me to the store when my father needed me so badly. It just seemed to me like my brother-in-law could have gone to the store so quickly in the car. It just did not seem right for me to be going to the store. I was hurting so not to be there with Dad while he was doing poorly. I was really frustrated. But I went to the store anyway and got the Epsom salt. When I got back home, Dad was gone. He died while I was gone to the store.

Recently, I saw a show on television that showed children essentially as the head of their household (home). That show left me in tears as I remember how difficult it was to take care of my sick dad and myself. No one can imagine what these children have to deal with every day of their lives unless you had the same experience in your life. These children were from about age eight years old to about thirteen, as I recall. Actually, I think one child was six years old.

My experience with my dad being permanently bedridden started when I was nine years old. When he died, I had just turned twelve years old. When a child is in charge of a home, there are so many disadvantages. First of all, I could not help my dad when his condition became worse. I could not take him to the doctor, because I did not have transportation. Even if we had had a car, I did not have a driver's license. There are so many limitations that children have until it is next to impossible to get even the basic necessities.

Even the grocery store was over three and a half miles away. So I would have to walk or hitchhike a ride. Then I did not know if I was riding with a pervert, or not. Yes, there were predators when I was a child. They probably were not as pervasive as they are today. In fact, I am almost sure of that.

So just dealing with home problems were next to impossible; however, that was only part of the job. I had to go to school cleanly dressed every day. Then I had homework for school, and since I was an "A" and "B" student, the teachers most of the time expected more and much better work from me than some of the other students. It would have been impossible to do without backup and support groups. And I had my sister Elena.

Chapter IV

Aunt Callie

However, from the very beginning of this journey, I had Aunt Callie. Callie Hollings was a wonderful God-fearing woman who loved people. She was known to almost everyone as Aunt Callie. Not only was she known as Aunt Callie, many people called her Mother Hollings. This title may have been more descriptive since she was "Mother of the Church" in City Point; however, she did not restrict that role of "Mother of the Church" to church members only.

Aunt Callie was probably seen more as a village mom since she was as comfortable and dedicated to helping anyone in the community who needed her help. In fact, this is exactly what a church mom is supposed to do. So, as far as I am concerned, Mother Hollings or Aunt Callie, defined the meaning of "Church Mom" or "Village Mom" in the way she lived her life.

I am reminded here of a question my nephew asked his dad. He said, "Dad, you are always telling one of us, 'I love you more than anyone.' Now, which one of your children do you love the most?" Now, my brother-in-law and my sister had twelve children. His dad replied, "The one who needs me the most."

That is exactly the way Mother Hollings was about people in our little village of City Point. The person she loved the most was the person who needed her love the most. I was the object of that love for many years. Consequently, there were no hungry people in City Point that Aunt Callie knew about. She was there to help anybody she could.

From the very moment my mom died, she became my mom. I remember an incident that happened on Mother's Day Sunday. This was a very popular day of celebration in our church. Everyone honored his or her mom by wearing a flower. If your mother were alive you would wear a red flower. If your mother had died you would wear a white flower. Needless to say, most white flowers were worn by adults. When I went to church with my white flower on, the older children laughed at me. Now, it was humiliating enough to have to wear the white flower. Then to be laughed at by other children really made me feel terrible.

Aunt Callie hugged me tight and took me into the church service of worship and hugged me through the entire service. Meanwhile, she made all the children who were laughing at me stop. She even threatened to use corporal punishment if they did not stop laughing. From that day on, she was definitely my "mom". That is the kind of love she showed everyone who needed it.

Aunt Callie lived her life as if she read the "Book of James" every day. She actually did what it says. She was rich, even though she lived on governmental assistance of about a dollar a day. She had no bank account, but Aunt Callie would give to people who needed it, continuously. Giving to help someone seemed to be her goal in life. To tell the truth, this woman lived this way every day of her miraculous life.

You see, Aunt Callie lived by a very old principle. Her principle was "add by division." Many people say they have never heard of that principle. Well, I can assure you of two facts. First, it is a very old principle. Secondly, it works even today. The truth of the matter about Aunt Callie is that she was grateful for all that God had blessed her to have. She owned her own home. She had two children of her own, a boy and a girl, who were older than my mom. Her children were both grown when she became my mom. She also offered to adopt a couple of babies from unwed moms.

Besides all that, Aunt Callie had a great and wonderful hobby. She would order one hundred baby chicks from Sears and Roebuck each year. So she had a small chicken farm. The lady also grew some type of vegetables almost year round.

Mother Hollings was my living example of a twentieth-century "Good Samaritan." It was such a joyful and wonderful blessing to have Aunt Callie as part of my life experiences. I am so very fortunate to have had Mother Hollings as my godmother. This lady was incredible. She was definitely a saint. I am sure she was a God-sent person in my life.

Aunt Callie was so wonderful that I adopted her as my mother. I cannot imagine my life without her constant love and demands of respect. This godly lady didn't just tell me how to love and respect myself and others, but she showed me how. This lady was the Mother Theresa of City Point. Nobody could have shown more love for his or her neighbor than she did. She demonstrated how Christians are to love their neighbors. The lady was a true picture of whom James (from the Book of James) describes as a faithful witness who practiced Christianity.

While reminiscing about my childhood, one of my fondest memories is how Aunt Callie loved me. She mothered me, but did not smother me. She washed and ironed my clothes. She also made clothes for me to wear. She also insisted on me keeping my body clean. Aunt Callie loved me with the perfect CLAD. She showed consistency, love, and discipline as long as she lived.

She not only helped me, but she also helped my two brothers and my dad. She liked cooking our food for us. That was a great way to help Dad who really did not like cooking every day.

My dad's and Aunt Callie's examples of actual love gave me a pattern to live by. In fact, in all these years, it never occurred to me how much I am like my dad and Aunt Callie. As I said before, it just seemed like they were always thinking of how they could do some good deeds. Likewise, it seems that I inherited that trait from Dad. Nothing seems to give me more pleasure than helping someone who really needs and wants my help. And I thank God I am a giver and not always a taker.

I have developed a set of values from three facts as follows: Fact number one, I concentrate on the three L's: love, laughter, and life; fact number two, people are more important than property, prose, or problems; fact number three, which is in the form of a question, asks "What can I do today to make life better for someone else as well as myself, even if it is someone who may not deserve better?

The above statement of values perhaps sounds like antiquity. The truth is the concept still works today. Just as Aunt Callie's principle is old but still works, so does the statement of values listed above.

Of course, add by division is much more antique than Bindie's statement of values. For example, do you remember Jesus using "add by division"? Jesus used this principle to feed more than five thousand people. You know, that was really multiplication by division. As a matter of fact, Jesus used this principle more than two times. Furthermore, that is not the first use of this principle in the scriptures. The prophet, Elisha, used this principle in the Old Testament.

There are other instances where this principle is used in the Bible. So, you see, it is a very old principle that still works. I can understand why many people reject the idea. It does not make sense to many people, meaning, it is not logical.

Chapter V

Mae

Many things in life don't seem logical, for example, choosing a wife when you are in sixth grade. Still, it can happen. I know because it happened to me. After the surreal experience with my mom, I began to observe people and things more closely. One of my biggest observations or discoveries I made happened when I was in the sixth grade.

One afternoon, I was standing on the playground just looking around. And it happened when I was paying attention to this class of fifth graders as they were playing and running around. Then I saw her! There was this girl with the prettiest eyes I have ever seen in my life. To me, her eyes were so very pretty that they looked unreal.

Meanwhile, as I was watching this girl so intensely, closely, carefully, and long, it was as if I was charmed. It took me a while to see the rest of her. Her eyes were so attractive until I must have spent almost my whole recess period just looking at her. When I finally began to see all of her, she had this pretty, long hair. She was dressed in this beautiful dress with the bottom of her dress just standing out all around her.

I was still living in City Point; however, I was going to school in Cocoa, Florida. So this angel, this girl, was new to me. I asked one of my classmates who was this girl in the outstanding dress. He told me her name was Mae Hichardson. "Boy, she's got a real mean daddy," he said. "So don't do anything to her."

Then I wanted to argue with my classmate. It is not Mae Hichardson. I know Mae Hichardson. Mae is Matthew Hichardson's sister. Matthew's sister is not that pretty, I mean that short. She is tall. Matt's sister is much taller than this girl.

He says, "Bindie, that is another Mae Hichardson. "Hey, Bindie, are you all right? You look kind of out in space." "Yes, I am all right," I replied. I had never even seen someone as pretty as her before. "That is my wife," I said to myself. "That is the girl I am going to marry."

This girl was the prettiest girl in the world. She captured not only my eyes and my mind, but my heart as well. I just wanted to be with this girl. She is my princess in this lovely dress. This is my *knightress* who took me to another world. It seemed as if only the two of us were on the playground. In actuality, there were at least three classes out there on the playground that day.

This girl was amazingly attractive. I had this ambiguous feeling. I honestly could not tell if I was being rescued or captured. The oddity of it all is that it does not matter. I found out one thing about myself that day however. That particular day I found out how terribly shy I am. I wanted to go over and say something to Mae, but I could not. I was actually frozen. I was just too awfully shy.

However, before the bell rang for us to return to our classrooms, I finally built up enough courage to walk by Mae and say, "Hi". I was like a walking statue as I passed her. Meanwhile, I don't think she noticed me, at all.

From that day on, I had a better reason for going to school each day. I continued to study a lot. The school day was much more interesting, that is, if I could see Mae at least once every day. If I did not see her, I would have to go home and be a little blue and sad. Fortunately, I did not have that many blue days.

Part Two

Understanding Poverty

Binderella

Chapter VI

Circumstances Of School

I should have known I was being prepared for something. It was during that summer, after my classmate so formally introduced me to Mae, that my dad died. I then went to live with my sister, Elena. This was not a pleasant move at all, because my older brother, Tarmmy, lived there, and because I felt that feeling about Dad and me even more. Now that Dad is gone, I have a double portion of the family hate, my dad's and mine.

Meanwhile, that whole school year was very difficult. The teacher sometimes wanted more than I could produce. This was true in class work as well as other situations. I remember one incident clearly. In sixth grade, I made A's and B's all year long; however, my teacher told me I could not get promoted. This was because in order to go from sixth grade to seventh grade I had to participate in a graduation ceremony. Now, in order to participate in this event, I needed certain attire. So when I told the teacher I did not have the requited attire to take part in the ceremony, the teacher replied very firmly, "Well, you cannot get promoted to seventh grade." I could not believe what I was hearing from Mrs. Hord.

The issue became known to Principal Norse. He told the teacher she could not do that. He said keeping me in sixth grade because of my poverty was wrong. Consequently, somehow I was given the clothes I needed to take part in the graduation ceremony.

Those were the types of issues a child in utter poverty had to deal with. The teacher did not consider my side of the issue at all, until the principal told her she was wrong. The teacher just knew what she was requiring any parent could afford. Of course, she did not know what was happening in my home and in my life. I was in charge of my home, and I did not have an income to provide all of the necessities. I barely had the resources to go to school clean and neat.

Another incident happened to me after Dad passed away. As I said, I was living with my sister, Elena. I was receiving a dollar a day from the government. My sister could not handle the many visits by the government personnel. So my sister told her to discontinue my governmental assistance. Then a couple of events took place. First, the cafeteria lunch prices at school went up. It was so much my sister could not afford it for me.

Later, we found out that I could receive lunch free. So I could have "free lunch" from the cafeteria each school year. Oh, what a blessing, except the other students would ridicule me. I could not take it. I was too shy to accept free lunch. I had this feeling of shame and embarrassment for all of the teasing from my classmates. Children can be very hurtful and cruel without even knowing what they are doing. Then, too, some know and don't care.

Meanwhile, I began to look for a job to do on Saturday to pay for my lunch. I began by helping my older brother, Tarmmy, who already had some lawns he kept up on the weekends. It was his part-time work. As I helped him, he would share some of his pay. And I learned the lawn service business well from my brother, Tarmmy, who by the way had stopped stepping on me.

When Tarmmy felt like I knew enough, he let me take over one of his lawn service jobs. So I had my lunch money. My sister didn't have to pay it, and I was not on "free lunch". That was such a good feeling.

Now, when school started that next fall, I could concentrate on schoolwork and my Princess (*knightress*). I now called her my girl-friend, even though she didn't know she was my girlfriend. Besides my schoolwork, Mae became my only focus. I had to have someone to think about to keep me from missing my dad so much. By this time, my Aunt Callie was very ill.

During this time, I learned something from my older brother, Tarmmy. He told me that the reason he would beat me up so much was because he loved me. Does that sound familiar to anyone? I know abused spouses have heard it before. They are abused because of the abuser's love for them. I don't know how my brother heard that; however, I know it did not make sense to me even as a child, meaning it was not logical. That is the same as saying children don't want to go to school because they love school.

It is so surprising to me today to see that our high schools do not have a 100% graduation rate. There is so much being done in order that every child in America graduates from high school. Why isn't it happening? Does each child in our high school see the benefits and advantages of a high school diploma? What will it take to make all students in our schools understand and see the value of a good educa-tion? Where do we begin?

These questions may seem to have no answers. However, let me assure you that there are answers. I have tried all my adult life to tell parents and children how important it is to get a good education. You see, every child in America can grow up to have, at the very least, a satis-fying, if not a good or excellent life. I know there are no magical answers; however, there are answers. I am not naïve about this fact.

We had a very good start on this matter many, many years ago, long before the politics of "No Child Left Behind." One of our former presidents, an educator, gave our whole nation a good beginning. The man also gave us an excellent "road map" to getting each child in America a good education. Yes, President Lyndon B. Johnson's education programs and policies were a fantastic beginning of the road map to a 100% gradation rate for all of the high schools in the United States of America.

The education and equal rights programs were the heart of President Johnson's "Great Society Program". He said, "Education is not a problem, education is an opportunity." According to President Johnson, it is part of the American Covenant. "Here at home (in America), one of our greatest responsibilities is to assure fair pay for all of our people. Every American has the right to be treated as a person, and he or she should be able to find a job, and he or she should be able to educate his or her children."

So, to ensure this education for all children, it begins with "Head Start" and continues through the college grants and loans. Just as the president said, "This program is much more than a beginning. It is a commitment. It is a total commitment by this president and this nation to pursue victory over the most ancient of mankind's enemies. Let us, above all, open wide the exits from poverty to the children of the poor. Poverty has many roots, but the taproot is ignorance." It is the lack of knowledge and skills.

I can bear witness to the college assistance program. I am a beneficiary of one of the programs. So if a poor orphaned African American child from City Point can finish high school in the 1950's and go to college, believe me, every child in America can do the same. How did Bindie do it? He had only four things going for him. They were faith, actual love, vision, and humility.

I have this awesome feeling of ambiguity in me, by seeing so very many foreign children come to America and emerge themselves by taking full advantage of our educational system and opportunities. Meanwhile, an overwhelming majority of our natural-born children, children born in America, are repulsed by the opportunities. What will it take to reverse this attitude of repulsion to school by so many American students?

I suppose that my view of our students' lack of motivation to be the very best they can be is swayed since so many children in my generation and prior generations were stuck so badly in utter poverty. There was absolutely no chance of rising above that poverty level.

Every now and then or once in a blue moon, a person in our poverty-stricken community would get a chance to show his or her outstanding talent or ability. However, there was not much giving back to the community.

From the background of poverty, perhaps I see students' opportunities today through the eyes of foreigners, people who are coming to America from poverty-stricken countries. These folks can see a land of opportunity. To these people from outside the United States, this nation is a paradise, even school. You can get anything you want. There are three magic words: study, work, and save. All you need to do, as a young citizen in this nation to be a success, is to study and complete high school, work to make some money, and save some of that money. Don't waste your resources and don't be stuck "SIS" (stuck in stupidity).

Chapter VII

Our Society

I suppose the difference in the view of incoming citizens and those born in America is just two words. The words are vision and hope. I have been told, "There are none so blind as those who would not see." When a person comes from utter poverty and one can see hopefulness and feel hopeful, then that person can have a vision of a good life.

We have so much materially in this nation of the United States. It seems as if we take everything for granted. The value of people and things do not seem to be holding up. In other words, our society has devalued everyday and everything. The primary loss is moral values. So that is the reason for our children placing education so far down on the list of needs. Everything has to have instantaneous or immediate gratification or it is not valuable. If I don't need it right now, then I don't need it.

That is not our whole society but a large portion of our society has this view. If I don't need it right now, I don't need it at all. So if I don't need an education right now, then I don't need one at all. We are so focused on the now that we have no acknowledgment of history or concept of the future; hence, many of us have no vision or hope.

It is very much like when the teacher told her student to study hard. He asked, "Why?" The teacher replied, "You will be able to take care of yourself and have your own place, etc." The little student said, "I have my own room." The teacher said, "What about when you grow up and get married?" He said, "My mom told me that is my room, and I will always be welcomed home."

Now, that reflects the lack of vision. This student does not see himself in the future like his father. He can only relate to the here and now. He may be blinded by all of the wealth of things that he has. Wherein, he should be having a vision of goals he wants to achieve beyond what his parents have.

This whole concept may be easier for people to see if they grow up in poverty. Children growing up in a land of extensive neediness would want and dream of more than mediocrity or penury.

When a person has hope, then usually a vision for the future comes to that individual. At that point, even a young child can get a true picture of a future with its overflowing opportunities. Some may call it faith or confidence about a good life in his or her future. Those amazing opportunities are so plentiful in today's world until it seems unreal. Again, however, there are none so blind to these great chances to have a good life as those who would not see it. If you close your eyes, you would not see. However, the time is ripe, for anyone who wants a good life can have it, but you have to want it.

The days are passed and gone when there was no choice. That is when the African American who was not a laborer was either a teacher or a preacher. In today's world, it is illegal to show open discrimination in the United States of America. In fact, if someone can prove a case of discrimination, it is a very good chance to win a lawsuit.

The opportunity for young people of America to make a good living and a happy life is so much better today. It is so much better than when I was a younger man that it seems like a different nation from the one in which I grew up. As a matter of fact, it is a totally different nation. Why is it so hard for children in the United States to see that fact? It seems so obvious until every child in our country should be upset with anyone or anything that attempts to impede his or her chance to get the best education possible; however, the situation is the exact opposite.

Chapter VIII

The Military

I sometimes wonder why these wonderful opportunities to receive scholarships, grants, and educational loans were not available to my oldest whole brother. He was very smart and gifted. Someone told me there are scholarships for left-handed persons today. That would have been perfect for my whole brother, Ivee. However, I have to remember that he grew up in the same period of racism and discrimination that I did. In fact, his chances or opportunities were far less than mine.

I suppose that Ivee tried to create his opportunity by joining the military at an early age; however, it did not work out the way he wanted it to. First of all, while Ivee was serving in the military, Dad died. Also, while he was serving his term in the military, he was wounded on the battlefield. Then he returned home in a state of shock. His physical or fleshly injuries healed soon after he returned home. Nevertheless, his emotional and mental state did not heal. I guess it was battle fatigue or something. It took years for Ivee's old or original mature personality to return.

When Ivee's personality did come back to him, he completed his high school education. When he finished his high school program, I encouraged him to go to college. He could have used the G.I. Bill, but he would not go to college. That was such a disappointment to me that Ivee would not go to college. If he had gone, I would have worked and supported him financially. Ivee had such a shocking experience in the Army, until I assume it was just too stressful for him to deal with college. That whole situation hurt me so badly, because Ivee was my mentor. I knew he could do almost anything he wanted to do. He was not only my hero, but thank God he was a great and most wonderful brother. He was my Superman!

I could list many things that I am grateful to Ivee for, but it would take too many pages. In his older years, I was so proud to hear he had graduated from Colgate in Rochester. Ivee was a great Board member. My hope for Ivee died when he went to New York as a migrant worker, but he did not fail.

Part Three

Bindie's Brothers

Chapter IX

Reverend Ivory's Story

The following pages were written by a professor at Cornell University about my oldest whole brother. They call him Ivory Simmons, aka, "The Reverend Ivory Lee Isaac." However, since Mom was still in Gifford when Ivee was born, she gave him the Simmons name. Meanwhile, Ivee grew up using the name Ivee Isaac. He was unaware of the name on his birth certificate.

IVEE IVORY
Born: December 31, 1929, Vero Beach, Florida

Reverend Ivory (Simmons) lives in Newark, New York. He is an officer and manager at LSW Industries in Clyde and serves a church in Sodus. Although currently not a migrant himself, Reverend Simmons maintains a strong interest in that group and has worked through many community organizations to improve conditions both for migrants and for those settling into the community permanently.

I can remember, when I came here there were many different crops. You could start in June and work right through until November because you had tomatoes, you had beans, you had cherries, you had apples, your pears, your prunes, you know, all of those things would keep you busy all the way through. And it wasn't like it is now. You know, you pick one crop, and then you've got to get on welfare and wait on the next crop. I think that's a bad set-up. A lot of people think that migrants make a lot of money, but they don't make that much money. If you counted up the migrant wages and compared it to a person who's making minimum wage, I think you would find that the migrant would come short in terms of his total year's earning. He doesn't make the money that a lot of people think that he makes.

I think that one of the things I learned in my experience with migrants is that they're hardworking people. I learned that I think the migrants should gain a lot of respect for the work that they do. I think people do not give the migrants the credit that they should for the hard work they do in harvesting the crops. I guess one of my real concerns is what will happen to our crops in the future if the migrant situation continues to fade out. Machinery has almost taken over harvesting the crops.

I also learned that migrants see a much harder time than the average person. They're uprooted. They're not stationary so that they can appreciate being a part of a community year round. There are a lot of disadvantages in being a migrant. I guess that's why I decided to not be a transient. I decided to stay because I wanted to put some roots somewhere, and if I was going to be in this part of the world, then I might as well stay here permanently instead of coming back and forth. I guess my other concern was about the conditions that I saw. I just wanted to do something about it.

You see, before I really became involved in the church I was one of those people. I had a lot of hate. I had a lot of animosity in me. It grew in me for years. For years, I hated doctors. I hated lawyers. I hated hospitals because of an experience that I had when I was twelve years old. And I found myself working with the very people I hated, and that was doctors. My reason for hating doctors was because of what happened to my mother. When I was twelve years old, I saw my mother die at childbirth right at home because we were poor, and she couldn't go in the hospital, because we didn't have the money. There was no welfare. There was no Medicaid at that time, and the doctors would not take my mother in the hospital because we didn't have money. So she stayed home and tried to have a baby… and she died during childbirth. And that period stayed in my head. That day had never left me. And, therefore, that experience made me hate doctors and made me hate hospitals.

But when I found the conditions of the migrants in terms of health in this area, I couldn't help but participate in the health program, because I could not go through seeing the migrants suffer the kind of problems that they were suffering in terms of health conditions. If I could do anything to make that situation better, that was what I wanted to do. So I found myself, as a Christian, as a minister, with a different attitude and with a different outlook on life, helping the people that I once hated because I wanted to help my people. I wanted to help the migrants to have a better health program. That's why I worked hard. I served on the health board for a number of years. I served on the Regional Health Planning Board, and I served on the Finger Lakes Planning Board. All of this is to make sure that people knew what I felt about health for migrant people. This is the kind of thing that you have to do when you feel that there is a need. You have to put yourself on the line. You have to put your actions where your words are. You have to let people know from your partici-pation that you are concerned and that you are interested.

When I first traveled around, most of the migrant camps were in bad shape. Some of the places were like you were living on the dirt floors. There was no concrete floor. There was no wood floor. Some of them were just like clay floors. There was no attic or ventilation in a lot of them. Because you have to remember a lot of the migrant camps were nothing more than ex-chicken coops where they used to keep their chickens. I lived in one myself. I can remember one year back in the 1950's when I was living in a migrant camp. In that camp, there was a snow blizzard, and I was buried. I mean, I was plumb buried under the snow for about two days. I couldn't even get outside the door for about two days. They had to dig a road into my apartment to get to me. The roof was covered with snow. I couldn't even see anybody. I could hear people, but I couldn't see anybody for about two days. If you think that isn't a frightening experience, I'll tell you it is. A number of my friends were out as they were living up on a higher part of the camp. They were able to get out. They dug me out. That was in 1959.

When I came to New York, there weren't very many year-round people living there. In the 1950's, you could almost count the people, particularly black people, the migrants, if you wanted to, on your hands and feet. As the group began to grow, the problems began to grow. What was happening was that when the migrants began to stay year round, they were living in old houses, either old chicken coops that were converted over to camp houses and old rundown trailers, mobile home types. As the number of migrants settling out of the stream grew, there became more and more problems. I was already here and settled in the community. I began to see some of the problems. I became the vice-president of the Wayne County NAACP. As the result of that, I began to deal with a lot of different things. My first real initiation into dealing with migrants was I worked with a church group in Lyons that was called "Lyons Neighbors" put together by the Lyons Council of Churches to deal with housing, basically, and clothing for migrants. As a result of that, my involvement with the NAACP expanded my role in terms of community activity. We put together a county NAACP program which was called THRESH. The word THRESH was derived from different problems that were facing people in the county. We put it together by using the first letter of each problem with those problems being transportation, housing, registration, education, social problems, and health.

As a result, I found that if I could solve some of the major problems I saw, some of the other problems would take care of themselves. One of the major problems was housing and health. So I began to work with housing through a migrant program, which operated at that time out of Ohrman. A close friend of mine, Stu Nitchell, who ran the Rural New York Migrant Program at the time, zeroed in on health. We saw those as two of the major problems. We felt that if a person had adequate housing it would give them some incentive to work. And it would also pull them from outside into the range of the mainstream of employment, as they were living in camps on the backside of the farms with no transportation. Therefore, we felt that if we put them into housing in the mainstream of the area, they would be in the mainstream where they could get transportation to adequate jobs. So part of the housing situation would help solve the transportation problem. The other problem was if we got them into housing, they would have to pay a certain amount of taxes, and that would make them interested in voting. So we could get them registered for voting. Therefore, we got into a wide range of problems when we started dealing with health and housing.

Stu Nitchell was the initiator of the Wayne County Comprehensive Health Program. Through my endeavors, I established what is now known as CASH, which stands for Community Action Self Help. I organized that group. As a result of that, we brought in a lot of training expertise from Monroe Community College, Rochester Institute of Technology, Ithaca and Cornell just to do educational programs on motivation of people. So we were getting some education into the whole process, too.

Also, we found that people could not afford decent housing, working on the farm, seasonal work or whatever. So, one of the things we started to do was to initiate ways of integrating people into the industry through the Wayne County Rural Ministry, for which I was chairman of the board at that time. We brought VISTA volunteers into the county, and we had them assigned to all these different projects that were a part of the THRESH program. As a result of that, we began to make inroads into Xerox. Many of the people didn't have transportation. They were taken to Xerox by VISTA volunteers who transported them there and waited on them sometimes if the weather was bad and they didn't want to travel back. Some of the VISTA volunteers would even sleep right there on the job until their eight hours were over and bring them back home. That's the extent that they were interested in doing job development.

Before I got into CASH, I worked at Garlock Industries in Palmyra, and I happened to be the first black person who ever worked at Garlock. I became president of the union. As a result of that, my supervisor asked me if there were any more blacks that I thought would fit into their program. So we got about fifty blacks hired at Garlock through that process. Some of them stayed at Garlock. Some of them left after we effectively opened the doors at Xerox. They went to Xerox because it was better pay and better benefits. Some left Garlock to go to Mobil Chemical. So they spread out into all different jobs. So all of this was as a result of what we were doing in health and housing programs, because there were a lot of fringes that rode on the tail of housing and health.

And then we decided that we were going to build some housing. So that's when we started the self-help concept. We gathered about eight families. And I applied for technical assistance monies from Farmers Home Administration and from the migrant program we got grants to operate. Before that, I was operating off my own money. I was paying my own gas expense and my own telephone bills and whatnot. Then we got the grant. And we began to organize with the VISTAS. I used them as outreach people as we didn't have money for other outreach people. We organized the families and went through the whole process. And it was a process. I guess all of this that I have been talking about was up to about 1968 when we really got heavy into the housing part of it and got into the health area in 1969. That's when we started to establish the Wayne Comprehensive Health Program with Stu Nitchell. We both were working under Wayne County Action Program at that time, because there were no separate organizations until we established the comprehensive health program. Then we established the CASH program. Then those two programs spun off from Wayne County Action Program and started their own board of directors. As a result of that, they're separate agencies now.

There's always been a problem with migrants or blacks in this area in terms of housing conditions and particularly when you talk about renting adequate housing in a heavily populated area, which is predominantly white. I can remember a number of times we had human rights violations. We took people to court for human rights, and we won a number of cases because of discrimination in renting housing to blacks. So there was a problem. It was not always whether a person could afford it. It was just that they were black, so they were denied decent housing. That was one of the reasons why we decided maybe we ought to build some houses in order to make sure that people had homes.

It's strange because a lot of people thought that I was out of my place in terms of trying to establish a housing program. One of the prejudices in housing was that when we talked about building houses, they thought we were talking about building some more shacks, because there had been some shacks built in one area. When I say shacks, I mean inadequate housing built in an area.

And they thought that's what CASH was going to do. So a lot of folks were so hostile to the housing program that we had to go to court in some towns just to get a building permit. We had to have lawyers to get building permits in some towns because people thought we wanted to build shacks, and they couldn't understand how non-skilled people could build an adequate decent house. And that's what they were fighting.

But we went to great lengths to make sure that what we built was good housing. I think that if you go around the county today, I could show you some of the houses, and you couldn't tell them from contracted houses. So, in the beginning, we had a problem getting permits to build. After we started to build, some of the problems disappeared, because we were building good houses. There has always been a certain amount of discrimination in terms of changes for migrants, a minority people in this county.

I remember it was in the national news about Bobby Kennedy when he went to Wayne County. He was invited here by some of the groups that were working with migrants. And when he came to Wayne County, he went to the DeBadts farm in Sodus. That's where he was threatened with a shotgun to get off that property. Mr. Debadts was threatening Mr. Kennedy that he had no right to be here and he wanted him off his place. And he had some horrible mobile homes. You could walk in and the floor was rotted out, like woodchucks and rats had been sleeping in there in the winter and gone up through the floors. They were rat-infested. They had no inside bath. They used to have to go outside to shower and then come back in.

When I was doing the housing program, we used to take a lot of slides. And we used to do a lot of slide presentations to different groups on the housing conditions. I happened to be looking at some of my old slides the other day. I still have some of them hanging around home. And I was looking at some of the conditions, some of the pictures that we took back there. So what I'm saying is, I got pictures to sort of substantiate some of these things.

I can remember one year we got so hot on migrant housing because of the Cornell farm over on the lake. They had showers, but people had to walk away from the camp and take a shower and walk back to the camp. And it gets kind of cold, you know, in October and November. And they were putting the pressure on Cornell.

I know one week we went over there to the camp, and three days later, it didn't look like a camp ever existed. They tore the camp down over the weekend and bulldozed everything just as smooth and straight, like there never was a camp. They went over there before the state could get there and get on their case. As a result of that same situation, with the pressure that was being made, we went down and we boycotted the university, and we talked to the Dean. We made a lot of impact there, and that's where the migrant program originated.

The incident with Cornell is one of the reasons why we have the migrant program today. I know Karen Tobin was head of the migrant program at that time. This was back in the early 1970's. That was an interesting experience for us, because we were going to expose it. We were going to put it in the papers and on television. But when we went back to do that, it was gone. We were going to say that a training institution was housing migrants in this fashion. What do you expect from anybody else? And we never got a chance to really do what we were going to do.

A lot of people today see what I do, where I live, where I work and the things I'm involved in. They don't understand where I came from either. I lived in a place one winter when I first came home, a house over on Preemption Road where Fremouw Camp is. I lived right down from that camp by Fremouw's father's house where the little house used to be next to his father's place. I think it's burned down now. I lived there in the winter. We used one room all winter long, because we couldn't keep it warm. I heated with a hot plate, and I cooked on a hot plate all winter long. I didn't have much food, and I refused to go to welfare. So whatever little money I could pick up trimming trees is what I lived off during the winter months.

Back in those days, they had what they called cheap hamburger and cheap neck bones. We could get hamburger for ten cents a pound. I used to buy myself a batch of ten-cent hamburger, ten-cent neck bones, some rice, and some black-eyed peas, whatever… some old soul food. That's what I lived off during the winter months. And I cooked it all on a hot plate. I didn't have an adequate stove. I couldn't afford to buy bottled gas, but they supplied the electricity. So I used the electricity and heated with the hot plate. We lived in one room with the hot plate. And that was how I survived with food, cooking, and heat.

I don't believe that our system should establish a welfare system that will let people sit down and not work. When I grew up, my father worked. They had what they called the WPA.

The Works Projects Administration was a program that was established during President Roosevelt's era, after the Hoover days. It was a work program designed to employ people who were unemployed. They made such jobs so they could go out and help repair the highways or the roads and streets.

My father worked on what they called the mosquito control under the WPA. Mosquitoes were bad in Florida. The workers would go out across the swamps, and they would cut ditches across swamps so that the mosquitoes would flock to the ditch. They would go along and spray the ditches and that's what killed the mosquitoes. That was called the mosquito control. You have to appreciate the fact that cutting ditches across swamps was a dangerous business. There were rattlesnakes, moccasins, and all those kinds of things. They did that kind of work for the WPA to earn $9.75 for six days a week, ten hours a day. This was right after the Hoover days that I saw my father work six days a week and bring home $9.75.

And people say, well, I can't make enough money to survive. But let me tell you something. I survived off ten or twelve dollars a week when I had to, because I didn't want anyone giving me anything. There are too many people who want things given to them, and that's why we can't get people to work today. That may seem harsh or may seem hard. But I think some of the cold realties that this country and the people in this country need to face are that if people can't get a job; there should be some way of finding work for those people.

You know, if I'm going to get welfare, it seems like our government ought to say, "Okay, where can we find some jobs that can be done so that I don't feel like people are giving me anything?" I'm working for it. If this means sweeping the street, at least I can say, Hey' I'm earning this, and give me some pride in my living and in my survival." I feel like that's important.

I picked oranges when I was young, but I didn't like picking oranges. So when I was fourteen, I started loading fruit before I went to picking… I guess I was fourteen or fifteen years old. I was born in Vero Beach, Florida. That's in Indian River County, which is the home of the Brooklyn Dodgers.

I'm one of seventeen children. I have fifteen brothers and sisters that are still living, fifteen including myself. We were raised in a small town, a little place this side of Cocoa Beach called City Point, a little small town. I was raised in this small town, but there was no farm. There was a lot of fruit, but not on farms.

We went up to seventh grade in our school in the country, a country school. We were then transported from there to town by bus to school. So busing is an old game. It's true that in some places the children had to walk about two miles to even catch the bus. When I rode the bus, we had one bus that serviced about four towns, and there were about twenty-five miles of area that one bus had to cover. That bus picked up kids from all the towns. We all went to one school. So when I was in the eighth grade, I went to the high school in Cocoa. It was called Monroe High, at that time. It was there that I learned a great deal about other parts of the world.

I first started living in New York in 1954. I came to Lyons from the Adirondacks where I had been working during the summer. I was working in a restaurant. I came here to visit my brother who came here the year before and decided to live in western New York. So, when I came to visit, he encouraged me to stay, and I did. He was the only one in my family that was here. Unfortunately, now I am the only one that's up here except my own family.

I have five children. I have a son who is twenty-two, a daughter who will soon be twenty, a daughter who is sixteen, a son who is fourteen, and a son who is eleven. They all live in the area. My oldest boys' name is Haywood, and my oldest daughter is Denise. The sixteen year old, which is the next oldest daughter, is Glenda Riche. We call her Richea. And then I have a boy who is fourteen. His name is Ivory Joseph, his real name, after my father. Then I have my eleven-year-old whose name is Jamie. Around Newark he is known as O.J. My two boys play Little League Football. So he has a little nickname. They call him O.J. because of his real name, Ovit James. They love playing Little League football. So it's one of their things.

I work for a company now, which is called LSW Industries. We established the company as a result of the civil rights movement in the 1960's. My boss, who is president, knew me. I was heavily involved in the community activities. His church put on a seminar trying to understand the race relations in this country, and I was invited as the pastor.

At that time, I was pastor of the Mt. Zion Church in Lyons. And he asked me to come and do some seminars about black history. As a result of that, we formed an alliance. We established the company, which is called LSW Industries in Clyde. It's a pallet factory.

The company was established by my boss, my boss' brother-in-law, and myself. We were the incorporators. The "L" is for Luerssen, the "S" is for Simmons, and the "W" is for World. But that also matched our slogan for the company, which was "Learn, Stay, and Work." So it held a two-fold meaning. It was designed to hire and train migrants and disadvantaged people on the basics of labor working.

Many migrants never worked on an eight-hour job, five-days-a-week kind of a system. They had always been able to pick their hours to work, whatever they wanted to, whenever they wanted to, in the fields. When they dropped out of the stream, there was no real opportunity for those who were not on an educational level to get jobs. If they couldn't fill out applications and answer all the questions, their application was put on the bottom of the file. I know this for a fact, because I experienced this when I was with Garlock. If you didn't have a twelfth-grade education, you didn't get a job at Garlock.

Therefore, people that were coming here from Mississippi, Alabama, and Florida who didn't have a high school education didn't have the chance of a snowball in July. And LSW was designed to work with those kinds of people. When we incorporated LSW, we built into our incorporation the language that we would hire, train, and establish disadvantaged migrant and handicapped people. And we tried to hire those kinds of people in order to fulfill our commitment to the community and to our society. That's what LSW is.

We make pallets and apple bins, big bins that you pack apples in. At this plant, we also make what we call corrugated boxes, collapsible boxes for Fisher Body and General Motors in Syracuse. We ship some to Syracuse. We ship them to Ohio, Rhode Island, to the Tupperware Company in Rhode Island. We make boxes for those companies. So that company was established as a result of my church work.

But I should mention that from my time in childhood, I had left the church. I kicked the church when I was sixteen years old, because they said I was going to be a preacher when I was sixteen. And my church had established my seminary training. But I didn't want to be a preacher. So I left the church. I didn't put my foot in the church from the time I was sixteen until I was thirty years old. I wouldn't even go to church because I didn't want to be a preacher. I went overseas. I spent time in Korea and everywhere. I traveled all around the world, almost. And I still wouldn't go to church. And after I started working with the church here, I got heavily involved and found myself thrown into the church more than I intended to.

In 1960, I got the calling of the ministry. I didn't start the church I was with, out in the country in Lyons. It began as a place that was built for migrants for a seasonal chapel. It was built back in the early 1950's. It was a seasonal place where the migrants would go to chapel on weekends. And eventually we became involved in the church. A friend of mine, who was a migrant and went back to Florida, came back, and then we started the church. I became involved with the church in 1959. A close friend of mine was a pastor. His name was David Knight. I began to help him establish the church, at that time.

As a result of that, I got heavily involved as pastor of the church in Lyons. When I started with the Mt. Zion church, we began with a handful of people. I think that, when I left, once the church in Lyons was established, they had 160 members. We bought the edifice there. I felt that I had finished my work there and I resigned in 1974. As I resigned from there, I just stayed away, and I began to fellowship with the church here.

We came here to Sodus, and there were a handful of people, about seven people. And right now we have somewhere around eighty. This congregation here is made up mostly of people in this area, most of them ex-migrants. We have a number of little kids that come, and so forth. This church was established basically to work with migrant children.

The McClouds, Reverend and Mother McCloud, established this church and primarily wanted to work with the young folks, the young migrant kids. They wanted to teach them the Bible. That was the purpose of this church, in the beginning.

When I came here, this church was struggling. They had a lot of little kids here, but they didn't have many adults here to pay the bills and so forth. That's where I came into the picture. I began to work with the adults and began working in the community. People began to come, and the church grew from that. So that's an experience I've been able to enjoy. I guess God gave me a gift of loving, caring and dealing with people. So I guess it's one of those things that I enjoy doing. And God has blessed me to do that.

One of the things that I find to be significant about blacks in America is that most people don't realize that the church isn't given the credit that every advantage and every opportunity open to blacks in this country today, came from the church. It stemmed from their Christian faith.

If you look back at history, you will find every uprising from slavery to today to be rooted in the Christian faith. When you look at history, most of your politicians and leaders started out from the church. Most of your black politicians today are Christian-oriented people, even starting back with Adam Clayton Powell, one of the first black congressmen in this country and a pastor at the Abyssinian Baptist Church in New York City. He was a preacher. If you look at the Civil Rights Movement and look at the force behind the Civil Rights Movement in the 1960's, it was from the church. It sprung from the church, from Martin Luther King, the black man, a pastor. I mean all of the activity that you see that will help progress basically, springs from the church.

There was a time that there were no leaders in the black community, but the pastors or the preachers. As I grew up, there were only two types of people who were respected in the community as leaders and that was the black pastors and black schoolteachers. They were the leaders. They were the instruments of movement for black folks. And today you will find that the church is the root of all your movement because of the faith and the belief that blacks have in justice and freedom and in opportunity. All of these things are rooted into the black church history.

Also, I must say that I think education today is inferior to education when I went to school. I think we had a better education system during the early years than we have today. I think education was on a higher scale, as far as blacks are concerned. And I think blacks are being cheated in their education today, especially since we have integration of schools. I think blacks got a better education in a segregated school system simply because I think black teachers took time to make sure black kids learned what they should have learned. They didn't pass them on.

I think the school system, when I went to school, was much more in tune with the "Three R's" than they are today. It's funny because I look at children today when they're in ninth, tenth, and eleventh grade. Some of them can hardly write their name or spell it. We may have more involvement in social things than kids had when I was going to school. But I think the migrant system in New York State, in regards to migrant education, is much to be desired. It's tough on the migrant kids being transported from one place to another and to have them go there and have somebody say, "Well, you're going to have to be put back a year, because you don't meet all the academic standards." This is a put-down to migrant kids in a sense.

So, I think that the educational system of migrants really leaves a lot to be desired in this area. I've never been completely sold that the migrants get a fair shake in the education system.

And I think that what young people have to do today is to not just talk about conditions. They have to go about changing conditions; and you change conditions by participation. One of the worst things for young folks today is to tell themselves they don't need schooling or they can drop out, or to say they can make it. Well, we need educated young blacks. We need young blacks who can stand up and participate in the system, because you cannot change the system from outside; you have to be on the inside, in order to change the system. And this is what young blacks today need to realize, that if they can get inside the system, they can help change it. But from the outside, you can't change it; and I think that's the most important thing for young people today.

The other thing you hear everybody say is that you need to get a college education. That's true if that's for you; but if the person is not going to get a college education, there are many trades in this country that can be mastered by people who have the intelligence, the ability, and the desire to work in those trades. Carpentry, plumbing, and mechanics are trades of integrity. And many young blacks today feel that they have to fail because they can't go to college, but there are trades that are paying more than college-educated professions. You can become a plumber and make more than you can as a school-teacher, a personnel man, or many of those other positions.

And these are things I think are important; that blacks do not get trapped into the system that says you've got to have a college educa-tion or you will be a nobody. It's strange, because working with the BOCES program, they were saying to me, "You know we're going to have to shut down some of our plumbing courses, some of our heating courses, and our electrical courses, because people don't want that anymore; they think that's dirty work." What's going to happen? You're going to always need heat, you're going to always need some electrical work, and you're going to always need plumbing, and people pay for that. And I think that everybody's not designed for that, but they are capable of doing manual things. And I think that's what we need to look at.

I hope that our younger generation would really think about their contribution to this society. Let me also say that I was raised in an environment that said if you didn't work, you didn't eat. And that was the motivating factor for me when I was faced with a crisis situation, that I would not go to welfare. I've been in this state for thirty-one years. I've drawn unemployment for six weeks out of thirty-one years. I have never signed for a welfare check. Now, when people tell me that they can't find a job, it's either because they don't have the desire or they don't have the necessary tools. And if they don't have the neces-sary tools, then it's our responsibility, as citizens of this country and as taxpayers, to provide them with the necessary tools. And that's how I feel about our system.

Chapter X

My Brother Tarmmy

My other whole brother, Tarmmy, was not big on academics or school. He liked doing physical or manual work, more than academics. He liked working with his hands. Tarmmy was not lazy. He was anything but lazy. He was different from me. I loved reading and studying more than working with my hands. Whereas our brother, Ivee, received a double portion of our dad's gifts, Tarmmy and I only got one half.

My brother, Tarmmy, with all his anger and meanness, was the first one to see that I got a bike. Tarmmy was a very fast worker. Therefore, he was always able to get work to make money. He liked to work with his hands. So he was always able to get manual jobs. Just as Tarmmy liked to work manually, he hated the academics of school. He must have been miserable in school.

So while Tarmmy put his heart and most of his time into doing manual work, Ivee and I did a great deal of reading and studying. It may seem like Ivee and I disliked work with our hands; however, that is not the case. The fact is we simply liked reading and studying more. I feel that my dad is responsible for both of our favorites. He had a balance of a love for doing physical work and a passion about reading and learning more academically.

But, as I said, Tarmmy did not like studying. He liked working. However, because of Tarmmy's dislike for academics, he quit school in eighth grade. It was typical of Tarmmy to do things in a dramatic manner. In order for Tarmmy to make sure he was not forced to return to school, he went and got himself two full-time jobs.

I have always admired Tarmmy's passion for manual work. As long as I can remember, he has always worked two jobs. If it was not two full-time jobs, it was at least one full-time job and a part-time job as well.

I still hold Tarmmy responsible for, or at least partly responsible, for my own work habits. Not only that, but I am very grateful to him for being such a good role model for me.

Now that Tarmmy is over sixty-five years old, he is still a fantastic work model for anyone. Having lost my parents at such an early age, I thank God for Tarmmy's example to set a correct pattern for my life's journey.

Tarmmy has survived an illness, which would have taken many people's lives; however, Tarmmy is a tough fellow.

Not only that, but my older whole brother decided early to set his goals for life. Tarmmy wanted a job. He liked doing a job and getting paid for it. The job did not have to be easy; however, it had to be something that he could handle. Tarmmy simply wanted to do his work to the best of his ability.

If Tarmmy was satisfied with his work, it would please any employer. I suppose that was some of our dad's value lessons we learned from Dad's bible teaching. If the job is worth doing, it is worth your doing it to the very best of your ability. Dad did not just tell us that. He always demonstrated that to us. Evidently, he taught all of his children that fact.

However, as I have also mentioned before, it takes a whole village to raise a child to be successful. So in the village of City Point, my home village, there were many others who are not on the Board who gave me lessons and inspiration for life's journey. I certainly cannot recall every person in the village that gave me an encouraging word. There is one person that I recall, though, whose first name is Bob. He could not read or write. In spite of that fact, I received this advice from him. First, decide what is right for you. Next, be sure it is right. Then, finally, go do it or get it. Don't let anything or anybody stand in your way.

Now, what was so surprising about Mr. Bob was even though he could not read or write his advice was sound. He was a railroad worker who knew a lot about life and how to make it better. Since Mr. Bob was illiterate, many people did not listen to him. Still, his advice was good and sound.

That is another point Dad insisted on. Everyone has the right to be heard. That is being respectful. Mr. Bob's advice has meant much encouragement over the years. For sure the names of many others who gave my spirit a boost will come to mind, as I write this short story.

Some of the incidents or situations may seem negative and sometimes are. Nevertheless, many times we must take those negative incidents that we may observe and let them serve as positive lessons. We can learn from someone else's mistakes so that we don't make the same mistake. Remember the definition of insanity is doing the same thing over and over and expecting different results. Also, remember that you cannot live long enough to make all the mistakes yourself. So we must learn from other people's mistakes. We also have to face the fact that life is bittersweet. It is not going to be all sweet. Life is going to test our taste buds, figuratively speaking. All of us are going to receive some lemons, sometimes.

So we must learn how to make lemonade, or life will be bitter most of the time. So turn those lemons in your life into something good and tasteful. That is my way. There are many times when we get what we call lemons. And they are there to teach us specific lessons at that particular moment. One may become frustrated and/or aggravated. In the meantime, there is something in that bitter experience that is there to teach you a lesson, and you may not understand it until sometime later.

I am positive of this fact. If you question some of the people around, you will find that they have had the same types of bittersweet experiences as you have had. I have had so many bittersweets. I can remember several occasions when I surely thought the lessons could have been learned in a less difficult manner. However, I was always assured later that the lesson was needed in the very manner in which it was learned.

I mentioned earlier that I went to live with my sister after my dad's death. Had I not experienced that, there is no way I would be able to appreciate having my own place, as I do. "Momma may have. Poppa may have. Brother may have, or sister may have. But, you know you are blessed when you have your own." Not only did the experience teach me to value my own place, it taught me empathy, not sympathy.

There are several other lessons I had to learn through bitter experiences. For example, it took being surrounded by drunks while growing up to learn that I didn't need alcohol or drugs. People who are drunk have no regard for their own lives nor for anyone else's life. So, I had no need to drink alcohol.

On another occasion, I had to leave City Point, Florida and go all the way to upstate New York to learn that life can be better than what I saw in City Point. However, this trip with Uncle Ben, who disliked me, was a bitter journey, albeit, I made some lemonade.

All the way from Florida to New York, I kept remembering how Uncle Ben had so vividly displayed his hate for me. I recalled how, on this very rare occasion, I was able to play with my two cousins, Hemory and Shank. They went to my uncle, and he hugged them and gave them some money. When I went to him, he swung at me so hard. If he had hit me, I would definitely have been hurt. I had to jump out of his way. Then he began to use profanity with me. This is when I realized how much my uncle hated me. I never forgot that experience. And I never got close enough to him for him to hit me.

Now, this is the man I had to ride in his car with from Florida to upstate New York. He had not changed his feeling about me; however, he needed me. My uncle needed someone to work with him in the restaurant where he worked in Old Forge, New York. Why didn't he take one of those nephews he liked? They were not old enough or big enough.

This trip was literally out of this world to me. I had never even left the State of Florida before that. I had to forget about who was taking me and just appreciate all the sights. As we crossed the Mason Dixie line (south to north), I could tell a change in the way I was being treated. I was being treated like a real person. There was only one restroom for men and one for women in the public facilities. There was no sign saying "colored restroom." The restroom situation was the tip of the iceberg.

In New York, I was treated like a real human being, not like a "colored person." For that alone, I wanted to say, thank you, Uncle Ben, and thank you, Lord. This was fantastic, African Americans in Old Forge, New York, albeit only two of us worked at the Fern restaurant besides my Uncle Ben. That took some getting used to, because Uncle Ben looked white. So, the two of us felt a little out of place.

This was especially true, as one day I was going down the street in Old Forge. A little boy ran up to me and said to his momma, "Momma, he is dirty all over." The mother was so embarrassed. She just apologized. I said, "Ma'am, it's all right." She said he had not seen a colored person before.

Old Forge was all right by me, though. This place really made me see life so differently than before. I suppose, what I experienced was this culture shock. This place gave me a new view of life. I had at least three seriously wonderful revelations or discoveries. However, there were not any other experiences like the one above. Everyone was at least courteous and polite. In fact, there were so many positives that it was very difficult to remember many negatives. I really enjoyed my summer job plus all the benefits and discoveries that came with it. Even though, during the summer there was very little time for recreation and relaxation, it was great. I was busy working most of the time, and when I was not, that time was used for rest and house or room upkeep. It was during my off-work time I could appreciate those wonderful revelations and discoveries.

First, I worked every single day. Still, even though I worked everyday, I did not get tired. Then too, while working in a restaurant, there was lots of food to eat. So, for the first time, I did not even think about the next meal. That was such a wonderful feeling of relief. All I had to do was take care of my duties, and everybody treated me good.

Another discovery was that I could save money. In fact, I could save my entire paycheck each week. Our meals were free. We did not have to pay rent. So each week I would take my entire pay and deposit it in the bank. I had a bank account for the first time in my life. Yes, this was a different world than where I came from. I never knew things could be so good. I wanted to stay in New York; however, this was a seasonal job. We went up to New York in June and returned to Florida in September.

While working at the Ferns, it was like living at home. There was no room and board to pay, so all could be saved. And the habit of working and saving became a basic part of my life routine. It was later that I learned the double tithes habit. That is, you pay God, and then you pay yourself before you pay anybody else. So, my second revelation was how to use my money.

I really believe I learned the twice tithes idea from my second godmother. While living and working in Old Forge, I went into a gift shop to look for a present for my girlfriend back in Florida. While looking around in the shop, the owner asked me to do something for her. I did more than she asked me to do. So she tried to pay me, but I would not accept any pay. Evidently, that impressed her, because she became very friendly. She was a very religious lady who reminded me of Aunt Callie. I liked her attitude. Of all the white people in Old Forge, she showed me the most warmth and friendship.

I really did not know that a white woman could show so much compassion for a little African American boy from the village of City Point. This lady, Carolyn Popkins, was so nice to me that I really could not believe it. We became very close. I adopted her as my second godmother. Now, I had two godmothers. One was African American and in Florida, my Aunt Callie. Then, I also had Carolyn Popkins, a Caucasian godmother in New York. It was very odd.

This was very strange but nice, because about the only person I missed when I would go to New York besides my girlfriend was Aunt Callie. So, now that I have two godmothers, it made me feel a lot better. This experience also helped me to see that all white people are not racist. I was so relieved to see this. I had learned to see white people in a different light. This was a third revelation to me, thanks to Mrs. Carolyn Popkins.

For you who think that because my Uncle Ben took me that he changed his feelings towards me, I assure you he did not. Why didn't he take the nephews he liked so well? That is a fair question. The answer is simple. His other nephews were so much smaller than I was. I was rather big and tall when I reached my teenage years. Many times I was thought to be an adult. So Uncle Been needed someone who was bigger than my cousins were.

Not only that, but Uncle Ben needed a worker, and that worker needed to be mature. He knew his other nephews were immature. However, the experience I had received in taking care of my sick dad made me very mature and responsible. So Uncle Ben may not have wanted me, but he needed me. So he used his good judgment and asked me to go. When I agreed, it probably was the best decision that both of us could have made.

I know it was the best decision I could have made at that time. Accepting that job in New York changed my outlook, attitude, and my perception of life. I really feel that is one of the issues that youth face today in the twenty-first century. If these young people could get a broader, more mature view of life, their attitudes toward school and education would be more positive and receptive.

There are places in our world where parents sell children into slavery. There are countries where children still go to sleep hungry at night. We also have parts of our world where children have to pay to attend school. The only problem is the parents of these children have no money. These children have absolutely no opportunity to rise above their poverty of their homeland.

The only chance these children have to get out of their cycle of utter poverty is to go to another country or nation. That is the reason foreigners who come to our nation can appreciate and take advantage of the educational opportunities in these United States. The experience of living in a poverty-stricken place can help a person to easily appreciate any chance of relieving himself or herself of a cycle of poverty. However, a child who is surrounded by wealth and who has the security of a welfare system cannot see the necessity of a good education. That child can't see the need to go to school every day and learn as much as he or she can possibly learn. In many cases, the parents of that child cannot see the need. If the parents could see the need, it would improve the child's chances of seeing the need and seizing the opportunity.

I am reminded of the time I was working in this office. I was down on the floor doing some janitorial work. It was a part-time job. My full-time job was teaching school. In the meantime, as I cleaned the floor, there were these two ladies in a line laughing at me. They were laughing at me doing this type of work, but they were standing in a food stamp line to get food stamps. So, many times, parents do not know the value of education and earning your own money. Therefore, if a parent doesn't know, that parent cannot help the child to understand. The parent's help is so badly needed.

When I began working in New York, it shocked me to find out that many New York students could go to a state teachers' college free. My reaction was why doesn't Florida have this, or does Florida have this, and I just never heard of it? When I returned to Florida, I investigated and found that Florida did not have that scholarship program. That made me want to live in New York even more since I knew I did not have the funds to go to college.

When I was fifteen-years-old, Uncle Ben took me to New York to work for the first time. It was such an experience in my life's journey. I will always be grateful to Uncle Ben for that favor. It really helped me to see the possibilities for my life. It might have also contributed to my "Bumblebee-itis."

However, during the summer of each year I went to New York, I learned a lot that I did not know. It was almost like going to summer school. There were always lessons to learn. That, by the way, is a fact of life. There definitely are always lessons to be learned about life. That is especially true if you are a person who wants the best life you can have.

This fact about living the best life you can is another lesson from Walter Ivory. However, this lesson was re-enforced by Carolyn Popkins of New York. She emphasized that point to me as often as she could. I am very grateful to her and my dad.

Another person who continued to remind me to do my best was my football coach, Richard Lake. Although Coach Lake had a major impact on my higher education, he was not my first football coach. When I was fourteen-years-old, Coach Mims asked me to join the football team. So I said I would. That season, I got some of the roughest treatment I ever had.

However, this was another situation in which my size was a great advantage to me. I could be a football player. I started when I was in the ninth grade. So when I became a sophomore in high school, I had a year of experience. At that point, I became a first string player. At that time, I thought I was on top of the world. However, I had no idea how this break would turn my whole life around. You see, there was no dream I would play college football.

The big opportunity in my mind was to go on trips to visit other cities. When we would have out of town games, I could see cities that I had not gone to. When I first started on the team, Coach John was the assistant coach and the defensive coach. Coach John was also the basketball coach but helped with football.

In my last two years of high school football, Coach John gave up the assistant football-coaching job to Coach Lake. He was a graduate of our high school and had returned to teach and help coach football. Coach Lake was a very good college basketball player. I think he had possibilities for professional basketball. Instead, he returned to his hometown to coach basketball and football. Gosh, I am glad he did. He brought one of those "Blue Moons." Remember, "once in a blue moon," a person who became successful would return to his community and help someone else?

In this case, Coach Lake returned to Cocoa and helped me. He coached me a little when I was in eleventh grade and the entire season in twelfth grade. What was shocking was he sent me to Bethune Cookman College with a letter recommending a full-time scholarship. I simply could not believe it. I went to Bethune that next fall. This was one of the most exciting and scariest trips I have ever taken.

When I got to Bethune Cookman College and gave the football coach the letter, I found out the reason for my fear. The coach said I have already chosen my team. That was it, or so I thought. I went back to Cocoa to give Coach Lake the news. When I gave him my sad news about what the Bethune coach said, I knew just what he would say. He would say, "I am sorry." Surprisingly, he did not say that. Instead he sat down and rewrote the letter. He got it typed up and told me to make another trip.

This time he sent me to St. Augustine, Florida. I went to Florida Normal Industrial and Memorial College. This time, the coach was more receptive. He told me since I was so small he would have to test my skills. What he really wanted to do is test my toughness. I could understand his hesitancy to give a scholarship to someone who only weighed one hundred and eighty-five pounds, especially if this person was a lineman. I was a tackle. This is usually the heaviest person on the line. I did not mind being tested. My only complaint was why the test was so long.

I had one other problem. Coach told me that all his players had off-the-field jobs. He said the only jobs left were in the cafeteria. I told him I would accept it. So I was accepted in FNI&M College. I really did not think about the fact that I would have to work all three meals. However, when I had to get up at 5:30 a.m. to get to work in the cafeteria, I wondered if I could handle it. I did not know that it would be as difficult as it was, especially when one has to bus trays and dishes three times daily. I also had to attend classes and do homework, as well as daily football practices.

Meanwhile, football practice was definitely difficult enough. Every day after exercise, for a warm-up scrimmage, the coach would let me see if I could block or stop our two hundred and forty pound fullback. Our fullback was also next to the fastest player on the team. So my daily task was to face this big, old, fast player. I didn't know at the time that he was trying to make me quit and go home.

I must say that after going to three classes and working in the cafeteria and taking the abuse on the football field, I considered going home. Even after all of that, I ended my day out in the cafeteria for the third time that day after football practice. After all of that, I usually ended my day doing homework or studying until late into the night. Many times I would study until the next morning especially if I did not have an early class that day. To say the least, it was very difficult. Still, that was the only way I could attend college, and that was my goal.

Many of the citizens of the village of City Point, Florida laughed when I would tell them I was in college. By the way, I was the first person in City Point to go to college. I assume that is the reason people thought I was joking when I told them I was attending Florida Normal Industrial and Memorial College. I guess they were thinking how I was going to college since I was the orphan in the community. They simply did not believe me. I would laugh with them. I am so very grateful to Coach Lake for his great help. I cannot imagine what my life would be like without my college education. The amazing thing to me is that he had enough confidence in me to write a second letter.

In my graduating class of 1957 only three of thirty-two graduates went to college that year. I was one of the three. I finished my first year of college and made fairly good grades. What was so very surprising to me is the fact that I passed all my courses. That was the one thing I really did not expect to happen. Therefore, I felt very good about my first year in college. It was a successful experience that I could hardly wait to tell Coach Lake about.

The good feeling over my successful first year of college carried over into the summer. That summer, as I went up to Old Forge to work, it seemed quite different from previous summers. Even the trip to New York was more pleasant than the previous years that I had gone. That summer, I was also feeling on an equal level with the other college students working at the Fern.

The summer was great. I had another very unusual experience in Old Forge, New York. This summer we were able to go to church every Sunday. There were only two churches in town. One was a Catholic church, and the other one was Presbyterian. When I talked to my godmother about going to the Presbyterian Church, she discouraged it.

However, the Mac's were Catholic, and when they invited us to go with them, I said, yes. So each Sunday I would go to the Catholic Church, but I did not take communion. Still it was a wonderful experience for this country boy who was always told to wear your best clothes to church. I was from a Baptist background. So when the

Mass started and we had to get on our knees and rise up and down, I was surprised. Yet there were many more surprises. For example, they always read three scriptures. Then the sermons were less than five minutes long, and they took communion at the altar. The people only got the bread and the priest drank all of the wine, real wine, not grape juice. All of that was so different from what I saw in the Baptist Church.

In the meantime, the biggest difference to me was to see young ladies come into church in their bathing suits with a towel wrapped around them. Now, that was a shocker.

This was an event that gave me a totally different view of the church. It showed me that these ladies were attending church to relate to and praise God. It was not important what I or anyone else thought. In other words, a person's religion is between that person and God, and that remains true. So, going to the Catholic Church was a very religious education for me. I really thank God for that education. To continue my education while in Old Forge, I bought a Bible. Before that time, I did not know that there is a difference between the Catholic and Protestant Bibles. I was always told the Bible has sixty-six books. When I looked in the Bible I bought, it had seventy-seven books. I did not know what to say or think.

When I returned to Florida, after the summer was over, I took my new Bible to college with me. Now, Florida Normal Industrial and Memorial College was a Baptist supported school. So my religious professor condemned my Duay (Catholic) version of the Bible. However, that was not the most important incident of that school year, by far.

When I returned home from Old Forge, I got some very disturbing news. One of my brothers, Tarmmy, was very ill in New York. He had to go to a special hospital. In the city where he was in the hospital, we had no relatives. Now, this is the brother that all my mother's children thought of as their whole brother. Surprisingly, none of his sisters or brothers would go and see him. So I went to St. Augustine and explained it to the president of my college. He told me when I returned it might be too late to get into classes. I told him I would try to make it back before registration was over.

I went to New York to see Tarmmy. He seemed so glad to see me. I really think it lifted his spirit. We had a very nice visit. That did my heart good, also. Meanwhile, I must admit when I left him I was in a state of anger. It just seemed that some of the other relatives could have visited him.

Then I remember how it was with my dad when he got sick. All of a sudden nobody knew my dad. He did not have any visitors. So those two situations showed me an awful lot about people and how they do not care about you. Those two incidents of illness taught me a great deal about most folks who say they like or love you. There are so many people who say or pretend that they care about you. In spite of what they say, how someone treats you says an awful lot about how they really feel.

After the experience with Tarmmy's illness, I began to lose my faith in people as caring individuals. I began to think, *well, if this is how sisters and brothers treat the ones they love, then I am glad they don't love me.*

All of this experience with Tarmmy and none of his other siblings acting like they cared, bothered me. It cast dullness over that gleaming, actual love I saw in my father and in my two godmothers. There was this other side of so-called love to give me a glimpse of real human nature. It took this neglect of Tarmmy by his brothers and sisters to get me to realize that there are only a few Aunt Callie's around.

Most of us are only concerned about our own necessities. At this point, I began to examine real human nature, not just with my family but with people in general, especially all the ones with whom I must have regular contact. This is when I started to look at people's empathy measurements. What is a person's EQ?

Yes, what is your empathy quotient? How much do we care about each other? Do we really care if a person is hungry? How do we feel about a homeless person? Does anyone care? Is there any concern for those in pain?

Until that particular period of my life, certain thoughts did not occur to me. I did not think about the fact that there are only a limited number of Aunt Callie's in this world. Most of our EQ's are very low.

So, yes, I was a very immature young person. I had been shielded, no, spoiled by my two godmothers. During this period, I learned another sobering fact. I learned that everyone who says, "I'm saved and sanctified" or says "I am a Christian" does not necessarily have empathy. Yes, I had been naïve about many issues in our world. To me, before this, every Christian had to have empathy. After all, how are we going to love our neighbor as we love ourselves without feeling empathy? No, sympathy will not help us feel another's pain. So if a person does not love his neighbor as he loves himself, is that person a Christian? Either he or she is not or that person is a sick Christian. See, anyone who does not love himself or herself is ill. Therefore, that individual needs help if there is no self-love.

The whole subject of empathy is much more serious than it may appear at first glance. However, every person should not have to suffer my life's tragedies and problems to learn how to be empathetic. To me, it comes back to learning from other people's difficulties and mistakes. If not, we will do the same wrong thing we know someone does and expect a different result. Isn't that the definition of insanity? Christians are not to be insane people.

Meanwhile, I am leaving my main topic which is that I was hurt that my relatives did not go to see about my brother, albeit, I did learn from the experience. Still, I am very glad I had learned the serenity prayer, which says, "God grant me the serenity to accept things I cannot change, the courage to change things I can, and the wisdom to know the difference."

Living that way would make so many of us have a much better life. After all, it did not change the fact that no one Tarmmy knew went to see him. I could not make someone else go see him. I accept that, thank God.

Binderella

Part Four

Change and Purpose

Binderella

Chapter XI

Stepping Out On Faith

There are many situations that many of us would change, if we could. However, there are some circumstances we cannot change. Thus, we must learn to live with the case. I could not change the fact that my father and mother were both divorced from their first married partners. Still, I can try very hard to stay married to my first and only love.

I cannot change the fact that I was born into a poverty stricken family. However, I can work to have more than I had when I was born. The problem in making progress for many people is that they think poverty is a necessary cycle. Once you are born into it, you cannot do better. It is not very hard for some people to think that they are stuck there. That is almost how I felt at the end of my second year of college. That is when hard times came. When I finished my second year at Florida Normal Industrial and Memorial College, something happened.

During the summer after my sophomore year, I received a letter, which stated that my college no longer had a football team. Therefore, I no longer had a football scholarship. Well, I thought this was the final word. I did not receive any more information about the matter. So I returned to Florida from New York and began looking for a full-time permanent job. I could not find a job when I returned home to City Point. In fact, I could not find a job listed anywhere in Florida.

After a few months of looking, I called my brother in Rochester, New York. I asked him if I could stay with him until I found a job. He said, "Yes," and I left the next day. I did not want to stay in Florida until all my money was gone. So I caught the bus the next morning. As soon as I crossed the state line into Georgia, it became very, very cold. In fact, when the bus got to Savannah, Georgia, there was a snowstorm. That white blanket covered the ground all the way to Rochester. My bus arrived the next day, and I went to Tarmmy's place.

The next day, I went to the employment office in Rochester. I filled out papers to get a job. It did not matter to me what type of job it was. If it would pay, and I could do it, and it was legal, I would do it. I soon found out one thing for sure. There were no jobs for half-trained persons. I had only two years of college. So there were no jobs. If I had four years of college, then I would not have had a problem finding work. However, since my education was incomplete, there were no jobs for me. Sometimes, of course, there are people or a person who is just determined to help you. This was my case in that Rochester employment office. There was this lady who evidently had a very high EQ. After she found out a little of my history, she said to me, "I will find something. It may not be what you want, but I promise you, I will find you something."

I must admit this lady kept her word. After giving me a bible to read, she said to me, "Come everyday and wait." That I did. And before long she had found something. She placed me in a dishwasher's job at a motel's restaurant in Rochester. That may not seem like much for a person with two years of college, but it paid the rent for my apartment. It only paid forty dollars a week. This was quite a bit less than the fifty-six plus room and board that I was paid in Old Forge, but it was a job.

Believe it or not, it took six weeks for me to get a dishwashing job. I went to Rochester in January. It was the middle of March when I got the job. I did not think that it was that difficult to find a job if a person had finished high school and also had two years of college, but it was.

In the meantime, I found the answer to a question I had asked myself a long time ago. When I first saw my girlfriend, I wondered if she was a rescuer or my capturer. Now, I know the answer to the question. Yes, it took me a long time, but at least now I know. She was both. When my dad died, I needed someone to relate to, and she was there. She rescued me from some of the gripping pains of losing my dad. However, it was a two-edged sword. Not only did she rescue me, she also captured my heart. I could not stop thinking about her.

When I returned to Florida from Old Forge the past summer, the summer of 1959, I asked Mae to marry me. She said, "Yes." At that time, she was going to Jones Beauticulture School in Jacksonville. So we agreed to wait until we both finished school before we married. Meanwhile, I could not get her out of my mind for a moment. However, when I was having such a hard time finding a job, I was glad I did not have a wife. That feeling did not linger long after I got the job. I wanted to send for her. So, I did.

I worked at the motel's restaurant for about a month. Then I said I am going to send for Mae, and we will get married. I suppose I considered it for about a week and a half. I wrote to her and asked her to come to Rochester to marry me. So she agreed, and it made me so happy that I just screamed and cried. That is when I realized it. I had been captured. This girl had captured my heart.

Chapter XII

Making My Marriage Vows

Meanwhile, this was about the last week in the month of April. When she took the bus and arrived in Rochester, it was the last week of April 1960. It was such a delight to see her. The day after she arrived we began to arrange our wedding. However, I ran into a very embarrassing problem. I was too young to get married.

So I swallowed my pride and asked my brother, Tarmmy, to adopt me and give me permission to marry. He did and we went to get our license to wed. We then got some more bad news. We were told we had to wait thirty days after we got our license to marry. However, when I explained that I had to leave Rochester in a week for a job in upstate New York, the clerk referred me to a judge to get a serviceman's waiver. When we went to see the judge, he gave me the waiver.

On May 5, 1960 Mae and I were before the preacher at Mt. Olive Baptist Church in Rochester, New York. Yes, there were one or two problems. Problem number one was that my brother would not attend the wedding. Problem number two was we did not have the two witnesses needed. However, that was solved when the taxi driver agreed to be a witness along with my sister-in-law, Louise. They were both very kind and helpful. Now, we come to problem number three. The minister says, "I am very sorry, but you cannot get married today." You have to wait thirty days before you're permitted to marry." I said, "Reverend Whitaker, we have a waiver. Please look at the addition to the license." He read it and said, "All right, I will marry you." So he performed the ceremony, and we were Mr. and Mrs. Isaac. That very day we went to the bus station for tickets to Utica, New York. It was the beginning of our trip to Old Forge. We were going there to work at the Fern Restaurant for the summer.

On the fifth of May 1960, my bride and I spent the night after our wedding sitting in a train station in Utica, New York. This all made me wonder if I was measuring up to the term of husband. This night was one of mixed feelings. I was happier than I had ever been in my life. Yet I was so disappointed for not spending the night in a fabulous hotel. I began to worry about whether I have done the right thing. Is marriage the right thing for us, at this particular time?

However, when we finally got to Old Forge, times were not like it was in previous summers. The job at the Fern Restaurant was not as much fun as it was in the years before. My responsibility increased, both in my job and in my family.

My wife was sick. When we went to the doctor, we found out why. She was pregnant. And the doctor told me, "The joke is on her now, but it will be on you later, Dad." Man, was he right.

When Mae and I left Old Forge in September of 1960, we went to Syracuse. A cook from Syracuse promised me a job at a restaurant. However, when we arrived in Syracuse, we learned there was no job at the restaurant. Even the cook himself was not going to be hired. That was a very uneasy feeling to be in this big city with no job and no apartment or room to stay in. It was very unnerving.

The biggest problem was being in this situation with a pregnant wife. It was very scary. In the meantime, we found a very nice little place to rent, but it was very expensive. After that I went looking for a job. I was referred to the hospitals for a job as an orderly, a nurse's assistant. Memorial Hospital had no jobs. But when I went across the street to

Crouse-Irving Hospital, there was a job available for an experienced orderly. I did get an interview with Mrs. Voolis. She hired me on a trial basis, and I did my best. She then kept me in the position of orderly. Mrs. Voolis and all the workers were warm and helpful.

Still I continued to look for work, because the orderly job only paid forty dollars a week. Our apartment rent was two hundred a month. So our little savings from Old Forge began to disappear. I was not getting paid enough for rent, not to even think about food and utilities.

Mae and I had to do a couple of things. First, I had to find a part-time job to bring in more money. Secondly, we had to find a cheaper place to live. It took a little time, but I did accomplish both objectives mentioned above.

The hospital job was very rewarding, and I learned a great deal about taking care of, not only others, but taking care of myself as well.

Well, the results of what I did in Rochester in May of 1960 are reflected in the letter below. Here is what I think of forty-nine years later:

16 Miner Road
Yulee, Florida 32097
March 29, 2008

Dear Mrs. Isaac,

I am writing to you about a person. This is a person I know very well. You know Mrs. Isaac. This is a person I would like for my next wife to be a carbon copy of. This is a woman I love very much. I am talking about you, Mae Isaac, my darling, my life, and my bride.

Thank you for all the love and patience you have given me over the last fifty years.

Thanks for the four lovely children, and thank you for your friendship. And I am serious. If I ever have another wife I want her to be a copy of you.

I am so grateful to God for you. I love you, darling.

Your beloved Ben

Chapter XIII

Meeting Bob Mitchell...and Others

It is just so amazing how differently individuals view life. I am not talking about just positive and negative. Some of us see ourselves superior while others see ourselves as inferior. Still, others feel lucky, and some feel unlucky. There are people who say they know that someone piled the blessings on them. There are some who say they are sure their life is cursed.

I have met people who say that everybody hates them. Therefore, these folks have no friends, just enemies. It is so sad to meet these persons who would not recognize it if they see a true friend. There are so many individuals who feel that all anyone wants is to take advantage of them. It is so hard to explain that this is not true. You see, there are enough selfish people around to make that thought conceivable.

In my life, I have become acquainted with individuals who would take from you, steal, or take what they want, even if they must kill for it. Many people have no appreciation or regard for life, not even their own life. However, I am not judging, because as I write these lines, in many of them, I see myself at different periods in my life. Only for me, negativity is only a passing phase. It is impossible for me to be continuously negative or doubtful. I have come too far, been blessed too much, and have seen too many miracles happen to people. That view of miracles would or must apply to my life as well.

One person who made a huge impact on my life is Bob Hitchell. I met Bob when I first moved to Syracuse, New York. When I began working in the hospital where Bob was, one of the orderlies introduced me to Bob. He was a senior at Syracuse University. Mr. Hitchell had been in an auto accident, which had left him a paraplegic. He was left paralyzed in both legs and both arms. When we first met, he gave me a warm smile. If I were in his place (condition), it would have been next to impossible for me to smile. So, Bob impressed me when we first met. However, that was not the most shocking impression Bob gave me. He completed his undergraduate courses and received his B.A. degree. Still, he had not finished with his educational journey.

Mr. Hitchell enrolled in law school at the same Syracuse University. All during this time of scholarly pursuit, Bob could not get himself up and out of bed. He remained in the hospital as a patient. He had access to the university lectures, which were taped. Bob's hospital was only about a block and a half from campus. Consequently, his professors were accessible. Therefore, if he needed to get some clarification, it wasn't too difficult.

Of course, even though Bob was paralyzed, he was mobile. He had an electric wheelchair. It had a big battery, and he could ride all over the hospital by himself. So, Hitchell had a lot of independence, once he was out of bed. He needed assistance with bathroom agendas. However, Bob had a leather strap on his hand to assist him in writing. There were many ways and times Bob needed help, but he seemed to focus on those things he could do.

Hitchell was continuously planning and working on those plans. The man did not show any self-pity. He simply amazed me with his courage and his zest for life. I know he must have had many times when he felt low or somewhat discouraged; however, I never saw him that way. Even though I worked on the fourth floor, I did not see him every day because he lived on what was called fourth light. It was a different aisle of the fourth floor than where I worked.

However, anyone who worked at Crouse-Irving Hospital knew Bob. He was well-liked by most workers. So they would do as much as they could to help him. As I observed Bob do his projects, I would think, *is there anything too difficult for us to do, if we really want to?* While I was considering that fact, there seemed to be one characteristic that all people with disabilities have in common. They all have at least a little bit of bumblebee-itis. They do not know they can't do the things they do.

This was also true of another person I know. His name is Dunet, and he could drive a car even though he was paralyzed in both legs. That, however, did not stop Dunet from a good life. He got married. In fact, he married one of the most beautiful ladies I have ever seen.

In the meantime, we should know that the conditions that Robert Hitchell and Dunet Miller are not the only disabling factors. There are other factors that are very disabling inhibiters.

Another thing that inhibits people is the state of poverty. This condition obstructs the development and intellectual growth of many young children growing up in poverty and destitution.

However, just as those paralyzed people can have a better life, so can anyone who is born in destitution. As I have said, I can give witness to the fact that there is a way out of poverty. In addition, others have brought themselves out of the neediness conditions.

The most direct way to get out of the condition of poverty is education. I really believe someone else would agree. The following story is from the January 14, 2008 "USA Today" newspaper, page 7D. To me, this is one of the most touching and inspiring stories I have ever read. This article tells a little about the life of Ms. Valorie Lewis:

STIGLER, OKLA.

"Labels are for cans, not for children." It's a statement third-grade teacher

Valorie Lewis lives by. Lewis knows that society often places labels on kids, marking them for success or failure. As a child growing up in poverty, Lewis was teased by other children and was once told by a teacher she would never amount to anything. "We lived in a horse trailer for about a year and then moved into a couple of tents next to a creek bed where we bathed and washed our clothes," she says. "We got our clothes from the dump, and sometimes we didn't smell too good." Lewis, 39, shares her story with her students at Stigler Grade School, a rural school in southeastern Oklahoma with a high poverty rate. Unlike many others who can only sympathize with a child's problems, Lewis' words and actions come from empathy and understanding.

"Been there, done that," Lewis says when a child cradles his head in her lap, exhausted from sleeping in a car the night before. "I've never really known a child to come to school and say, 'I want to grow up to be a nobody.' Giving children an opportunity to thrive is really all that is needed for successful human beings," Lewis wrote in her nomination for the All-USA Teacher Team. "As a result of my childhood, my daily goal is to create an environment that will allow my students to grow, dream, and find their great purpose." Lewis draws inspiration from her mother. When her grandfather would bring home cans of unlabeled food, her mother would let Lewis and her sister pick one and make an adventure out of opening it to find out what they were having for dinner. "As bad as it was, we had the love of a wonderful mom. I see many children that don't even have that. That is why I make sure that they know that I love them no matter who they are and what kind of problems they may have." She hopes that if

her students learn nothing else, they learn to respect and value others, whether they are rich or poor, black or white or have a harder time learning than others. "I had a teacher tell me once that a certain child wasn't worth bothering with," she says. "That same child flourished when they found out someone truly cared about them."

Lewis encourages her students to seek out the positive things about each other through a weekly activity in which they draw names. Throughout the week, positive observations are shared. She also gives her students a chance to share their thoughts and feelings each week during Community Circle time. "Each person is given two minutes to talk about whatever is on their mind," Lewis says. Lewis also holds high expectations from her students academically. Last year, five of twenty students scored advanced scores in math, including one special education student whose life story is very similar to hers. "All that students needed was a little encouragement," Lewis says. "They are doing very well now." Lewis' students use a computerized Smart Board each morning for what she calls "Morning Munchers," using programs for problem solving, measurement and other math equations. She also holds the Brain Olympics, incorporating physical and academic challenges, such as: hopscotch, math and vocabulary relays.

"Her students are afraid to be absent, because they don't want to take the chance they'll miss anything," says former school counselor Rita Echelle. "Mrs. Lewis doesn't always tell them when she is planning something special, so they have to be there every day just in case." Echelle says the love and dreams Lewis has for each of her students doesn't stop once they walk out of her classroom. "When her classes graduate from high school, she sends notes congratulating and wishing them well," Echelle says. "She even includes memories she has of the year they were in third grade. Some of them have written her to let her know how much those notes meant to them. One *mother says her son still has his hanging on his mirror. I have no doubt there are and will be those who succeed in life because Mrs. Lewis believed in them."*

One of the most difficult things in the world to do is to love a person and help that person to become as fully matured as possible. Part of the problem is we don't know when a person has made it to full maturity or potential. Most of the time an individual is not sure of his or her own potential. Another reason that makes this judgment or discernment so hard is the emotional involvement. Feelings can cause a total lack of good reasoning. When one cares or loves someone so very much, it makes that person incapable of making a reasonable decision or opinion. Emotions can muddy clear decision-making or the ability to reason. So many times people make opinions underestimating their students' development and their potential.

This same fact may be applicable to self-evaluation of one's own developmental ability. So Mrs. Lewis is one person who gives a person unlimited development ability.

This is one important responsibility that parents have. All parents must encourage each of their children to do their best. This is not a one-time act. Children need continuous motivation to reach their highest potential. In fact, this job is so pertinent to each child's proper development until a child should have limited contact with anyone who is not encouraging him or her.

Chapter XIV

Life's Lessons
for a New Dad

Living in today's world can be so interesting and challenging. I am so grateful to God for all of the wonderful experiences in my life. He has been as much a part of my life as any of the Board members. God has been so involved in my existence until it sometimes seems a little self-centered. It may be more appropriate or perhaps more accurate in writing "my story" to say History (His story) in my life.

There are times when I could say in regards to Joseph, son of Jacob (Israel), I know exactly how he felt in his mistreatment by his ten older brothers. I can remember many incidents of the Lord's interventions in my life.

God's revelations have shown me how He can protect you and how He can give hope and vision. He can show anyone what people are capable of doing, good and bad. In particular, He can show you how cruel your family can be and, at the same time, how very warm and wonderful a complete stranger can be. This fact is so true until it seems impossible that we are made or created in His image. We are all His children. So what makes us so incredibly different? It reigns from family hatred to sacrificing love by a complete stranger. There are people who have a total disregard and complete disrespect for life. Then there are people who are completely unselfish and willing to sacrifice one's own life. However, when most of us think of this, it is Christ we are thinking of. Of course, needless to say, this type of unselfish love is exceedingly rare. That type appears about once every blue moon.

However, this is the type of love I have been exposed to. I saw it first in my dad. I also saw it in Mrs. Callie Hollings and Mrs. Carolyn Popkins. It was also evident in how my sister, Elena, took care of Mom's children after Mom died. Without Elena's help, I might have ended up homeless.

There were so many other trouble traps in which Bindie could have gotten caught. However, characters like Joseph were excellent role models. Still there were many living role models like my oldest whole brother.

While Dad was still living and teaching us values to live by, he was so wonderfully blessed. One day out of the blue, his three oldest sons came to see Dad. These are the sons he left in Georgia. They seemed so glad to see him and vice versa. He was overjoyed to see them all grown up. This was the first time I saw these older brothers. It was not only a pleasant surprise for Dad, but also an inspiration to me to know that they still cared about their dad. The most impressive of the three was my brother, Mac. He was doing very well. Mac was managing a large business while also operating a small neighborhood grocery store. He became a model to me, also. This image of a brother of mine who can do this told me I could do something similar. In that instant, he became my next hero. His name is Jonah Mac Ivory.

Mac Ivory was Dad's second son. It was almost unbelievable to see how much Mac a/k/a Jonah Mac was an image of our dad. He did not look like my dad, but he has a lot of my dad's ways.

Mac was now one of my heroes. He kept himself focused on the future. My brother, Mac, never lost hope in his ability to meet his goals. He was a manager.

I thought Mac had many more obstacles to overcome than I have. Therefore, what is there to hold me back from meeting my goals in my life? That may be the beginning of Bumblebee-itis.

For some reason, I could not forget that image of my big brother, Mac. I could see him often reflected in my memory standing tall with his expensive-looking suit and his sporty hat. He was the very image of success, for me. From that time on, my goal was to be as successful as my brother. So my desires and aims were focused and set. I stayed in contact with Mac. He lived in Tampa, Florida. And, as often as I could, I visited him. Unfortunately, that was not very often until I became an adult.

However, until I reached that time in my life, Mac was my role model. I did all of the things I thought I needed to do. I applied myself in school and learned all I could.

My study habits must have been noticed by my teachers because they all seemed to try to help me as much as they could. Even my coaches and the principal got the idea to help me.

When I became very frustrated with some of my family members, I did something very dumb. I went to the state employment office to apply for a job. The lady that helped me called my high-school principal. He came to the employment office and took me to school. He also gave me a job. I became a janitor of the elementary school I had attended.

For a short time, I wondered why the principal did this for me. Then I remembered the time when the whole school accepted a free trip to the carnival. However, I stayed at school. I had not completed my schoolwork. So I stayed at school and did my schoolwork. That seemed to impress the principal so much, until he had to tell the whole school.

So perhaps that is why he went to the employment office to rescue me. Whatever the reason, I am indebted to him. That is the type of treatment Ivee was describing in the schools during our generation. I cannot imagine a principal doing that type of rescue today.

When Mae and I went to Syracuse, we visited some churches on Sunday. After a couple of visits to this church in downtown Syracuse, we joined. It was interesting, and the members showed warmth and care. The pastor was a seminary graduate and was also loving and caring.

We attended this church for over a year. Then an incident occurred to cause us to want to change churches. The choir director wanted to wear a red robe rather than black. He wanted it so badly that he divided the congregation until 650 of the 800 members joined other churches. To make it worse, some of the members who knew that I was a licensed minister asked me to be their pastor. It was an insult to me. So we began to look for another church.

I wanted to avoid the same situation happening again. All I wanted was to try to take care of my family. This same incident could have taken place in another church. Meanwhile, I did not believe that my denomination was doing enough mission work. So I began doing a little research on which denomination was giving the most to mission work. The answer was the Presbyterian Church. The fact is Presbyterians were giving more money to foreign missions and local missions. Now, while this is true, I did not consider then that so many Presbyterians are so very rich.

While considering the Presbyterian Church, I considered visiting one. However, I did not need to consider it too long. Within a month, a person working in the pharmacy department at Crouse-Irving Hospital invited me to her church. I asked her what denomination it was. She said it was Presbyterian. So I said, "Yes, we will come for a visit." So Mae and I went to Westminster Presbyterian church. When we went, we both like it. We also liked the people, although it was an all-Caucasian congregation. They gave us a very warm welcome and asked us to please come back. It really surprised me. I am not sure why, but I did not expect such a warm welcome.

They also went overboard over Bindie, Jr. He was the star after church. Everyone wanted to see him. In fact, this was true everywhere we went. He was always the center of attention. Bindie, Jr. was our pride and joy. He was born in Crouse-Irving Hospital on February 4th, 1961. That was the day all the traffic stopped in the whole city. Thank God, we had the foresight to take Mae to the hospital a day early.

There it happened. It was the day in our lives that Mae and I had waited for so long. This was an awesome day for the two of us, the day of the birth of Binderella, Junior. My co-workers said I could not stop smiling. I could not visit them both. Yes, I was a father for the first time.

After three days we all went home and celebrated. Mae and I had a very good time drinking our strong, strong grape juice. Bindie, Jr. joined us with his very strong milk.

This was the first time I had a baby to take care of, since I took care of my niece, Trish. When I was living with my sister, Elena, she had her first baby. She worked long hours. So I babysat my little niece when I got home from school. Trish was such a good baby, until it was a pleasure to baby-sit her. I would take her everywhere I would go. Sometimes I was jealous of my sister over her little girl. Now, I was not jealous, anymore. I was a father now.

We were so grateful for Bindie, Jr. He was the joy of our lives. I helped Mae take care of the baby when I was home. So he grew to love us equally. He was such a wonderful child. I guess my wife must have thought I was acting strange because I was showing off my babysitting experience. I forgot that she knew I had experience in caring for Trish, my niece.

When I was babysitting Trish, I would go on dates with Mae. Trish was our chaperone so that we would not get in trouble. Trish was right with us. So Mae knew that I had experience in taking care of babies. However, I still tried to show off. I would do anything she could do except breastfeed.

We were both so excited about Bindie, Jr. It was so evident in both of our faces. It would have been impossible not to show our joy.

My joy was doubled because I did not work during the day. I had a three-to-eleven shift at the hospital so I could spend all day with our jewel, Bindie, Jr.

So, most of my extremely joyful time with Bindie, Jr came because of the experience I had received in taking care of Trish. She prepared me to enjoy our first child.

However, nothing prepared me for the treatment we received from the people of Westminister Church. They were so warm and caring. It was a delight to attend worship. Then, too, no one was as caring and helpful as the pastor, Reverend Comeara. He helped us in so many ways.

Reverend Comeara was very active in helping us find a nice place to live. We were living at the "Red Onion," and it was not a place we felt comfortable. It was too busy with the "good timers." He was also instrumental in helping me follow my dream to finish my college education.

Binderella

Conclusion

This short story is only Act I of Bindie's surreal life, albeit, if an orphan child from the village of City Point can finish college, what can a child with parents do?

If a quadriplegic can finish Syracuse University Law School, what can you do? Then, too, if a homeless high school young man with no parental help can finish college, can you?

You need a vision and the "audacity to hope." With those two activities challenging you, few things are impossible especially if you have a village or even a Board of Directors on your side.

Now, I know how Adam felt in the Garden of Eden, naked.

Bindie, A Bible Student

I am so glad that my dad made my brothers and myself students of the bible. There are so many heroic and inspiring stories in the scriptures. The lines of historic heroes are very long. The story of Abram and his long journey is a great test of his confidence and trust in God. There are so many other stories like Abram's trip to Egypt, Isaac and Ishmael. There is that exciting story of Jacob and Esau.

However, one of my favorites is Jacob's son, Joseph. It would have been so easy for Joseph to have given in to his brother. He could have tried to hide his gifts. He could have given in to his brother's pressures and not have used his talents.

The fact is that Joseph knew that God had something special for him to do. Through all his ups and downs, he still managed to be useful in the Lord's salvation of his family and the nation of Egypt during the famine. As I have read and re-read Joseph's story, it always reminded me of my own situation, albeit, there did not seem to be a strong hatred by his sisters. Meanwhile, his brothers' meanness and cruelness seemed overly sufficient enough to destroy a weaker person, especially if God is not protecting that individual. It is so very easy to see the Lord's hands at work in Joseph's life.

Hence, it should be easy to understand why Joseph is a hero to me. My life experiences are so much like his. It makes me very glad I did not, or could not, talk about my goals and dreams in my childhood. Otherwise, I could have had some jail and prison time, too. The stress and strain was bad enough without incarceration.

About The Author

Ben Isaac was born in City Point, Florida. He lost his mother at the early age of three years old. After his mother's death, he encountered harsh treatment from his siblings from his mother's prior marriage before she was married to Ben's father. To make matters worse his father died when he was 12-years-old. Then Ben had to go live with his siblings that resented him. He felt like they hated his guts. He was called all kinds of derogatory names, such as: dumb, stupid, lazy, silly, ugly, etc.

But, Ben was favored by a "Higher Power" that placed others in his path to help him. Ben finished high school, went on to college and got his Masters Degree in education. He taught school for 34 years. Ben received many recognitions, including the "Teacher of the Year" award", started a Little League Baseball team when blacks could not play with whites, but he included whites. After teaching for 34 years, Ben went to seminary for two years until his health begin to fail. His motto to young people is: If I can make it with all the hardships I endured and no parents, what can you do with parents and the love of a family?".

ORDER FORM

Please Mail Checks or Money Orders to:

Ben Isaac
City Point Books
P.O. Box 221
Yulee, Florida 32041
benjaminisaac@bellsouth.net

Please send ____ copy(ies) of *BINDERELLA*

Name: _____

Address: _____

City: _____ State: _____ Zip: _____

Telephone: (___) _____ (___) _____

Email: _____

I have enclosed $10.00, plus $5.00 shipping per book for a total of $_____.

Sales Tax: Add 7% to total cost of books for orders shipped to FL addresses.

For Bulk or Wholesale Rates, Call: 1-904-277- 4210
Or email: benjaminisaac@bellsouth.net

Binderella